The Art of
STAINED
GLASS

DESIGNS FROM 21 TOP GLASS ARTISTS

CHRIS PETERSON

GLOUCESTER MASSACHUSETTS

QUARRY BOOKS

First published in the United States of America by
Quarry Books, an imprint of
Rockport Publishers, Inc.
33 Commercial Street
Gloucester, Massachusetts 01930-5089
Telephone: (978) 282-9590
Fax: (978) 283-2742

Distributed to the book trade and art trade in the United
States by
North Light Books, an imprint of
F & W Publications
1507 Dana Avenue
Cincinnati, Ohio 45207
Telephone: (800) 289-0963

Other distribution by
Rockport Publishers, Inc.
Gloucester, Massachusetts 01930-5089

ISBN 1-56496-463-9

10 9 8 7 6 5 4 3 2 1

Design: Minnie Cho Design
Cover Design: Sawyer Design Associates, Inc..

Cover artwork credited as follows:
Front cover image: *Flamenco in Cobalt*, by Carl Powell.
Back cover images: *La Olas*, by Rick Melby (left); *Untitled*, by
	Kenneth vonRoenn (right).
Front flap image: *Border Scratchboard*, by Linda Lichtman.
Back flap image: *Space Series Tile*, by Liz Mapelli.

Technique photography by Kevin Thomas Photography, except for techniques photos for Larry Zgoda and Carl Powell, which are by Michael Lafferty Photography. All other photography credits are listed on page 143.

Manufactured in China.

acknowledgments

Writing *The Art of Stained Glass* has given me a chance to work with a host of talented and interesting people. All of them, from the artists themselves to the editors who gracefully lightened my load, contributed significantly to the book. But there are two people without whom I could not have completed the project.

Stephanie Graziadio gave me more support than I had a right to ask for. Her endless enthusiasm for, and belief in, the book, and her insightful critique tempered with a true friend's diplomacy were invaluable to me. She was always there when I needed her, and for that I owe her a thousand thanks and then some.

My son Sam offered an indispensable, light-hearted perspective that focused me again and again on what really matters. The book would have been a much more difficult undertaking without the opportunity to recharge my batteries in his delightful sense of humor and boundless optimism. I can't imagine a greater son or a better friend.

contents

introduction

I've long wanted to write a book on glass art. For fifteen years, I've held a deep and resounding appreciation for the medium and the artists who work in it. It is a unique material, and these artists are exceptional in their drive to overcome relative obscurity and make the public—and the arts community—recognize the distinctive potential of glass as an art form.

Glass artists inevitably fight an uphill battle for legitimate recognition, their works consigned to the less prestigious and less financially rewarding arena of "craft" versus the "fine arts." This has been a frustrating struggle to witness. A great painter must master the nuances of light and shadow, line and perspective, and generally must create meaningful, intriguing, and thought-provoking work to be lauded. A great glass artist must do all that in a less malleable medium. But the glass artist can never hope to stand on the same pedestal of public acclaim the painter occupies. I hope this book plays a part in changing that misguided perspective.

Glass art offers qualities beyond those found in other fine arts. One of the greatest challenges a glass artist faces—in addition to those that any visual artist must tackle—is the changing nature of the light that illuminates the work. In contrast to paintings that are usually lit under set and unvarying conditions, a work of glass is more often than not viewed in both transmitted and reflected light. A talented glass artist can make the inherent statement heard in all potential lighting situations.

Of course, the ultimate test of any great artist, regardless of medium, is the innovation and originality of their expression. That is what sets apart the artists in *The Art of Stained Glass* from so many others. I believe the reader scanning these pages will come to the same realization I came to so many years ago, namely that this is fine art. Artists such as Rachel Schutt-Mesrahi, Patrick Reyntiens, and Lutz Haufschild have created notable bodies of work that will stand the test of time as unique, enduring works that express relevant commentary on the natural world, architecture as living environment, and the human condition.

The Art of Stained Glass also offers the reader a chance to revel in the sensual, vibrant nature of stained glass. From the liquid appearance of textured glass, to the seductive, surreal tones of painted glass, to the riveting sparkle of beveled glass, the medium is nothing if not alluring. But make no mistake—although the extraordinary work shown here is wonderful evidence of the medium's potential, these artists recognize no boundaries in the forms or techniques of stained glass. They will combine, refine, and alter methods and materials as they see fit to create the individual statements they want to make exactly as they want to make them. They share the desire to use the medium as an ideal, and ultimately beautiful, vehicle for expression and communication. I think one look will leave anyone with eyes hungry for more. Let the feast begin.

STAINED GLASS
POWERFUL COLORS

Stained glass is born from the fiery drama of an oven so hot it

hurts just to look inside. The color and the drama become integral

to the glass and cannot be erased. Glass artists through time have

been drawn to the vivid colors and variations—mistakenly called

"imperfections"—in the glass. Lit by direct or ambient light,

stained glass panels have a life all their own, ripe with magnifi-

cent and seductive hues. Talented and visionary glass artists join

pieces of this material in a process called *leading*, placing each

piece in one side of a two-sided channel called *came*. The best

artist acts as a composer, creating a symphony with the material

and the lines that connect it.

Characteristic of the best stained glass artists, Rachel Schutt-

Mesrahi takes this enigmatic material in new and challenging

directions. Rather than ask, "Can it be done?" she inquires, "How

will I do it?" Sigrídur Asgeirsdóttir also stretches the bounds of

what many viewers traditionally consider glass art. As do all the

artists featured in this book, she challenges her audience to think beyond the medium's obvious properties to glimpse statements that surpass the material.

David Wilson produces larger, more architecturally related statements. Using a muted palette that includes colorless glasses, he strives to improve buildings with the transmutation of natural light. Rick Melby, on the other hand, works with artificial light. His interior light fixtures combine a range of influences, from Bauhaus Germany to traditional Japan, in unique sculptural designs.

Lutz Haufschild also creates architectural art, striving to achieve an integrity that goes far beyond the medium. He aims to instill architecture with an essence and a spirit that elevate the entire structure. Kuni Kajiwara shares that goal as she approaches her commissions with one of two styles—precise geometry or simple abstract design.

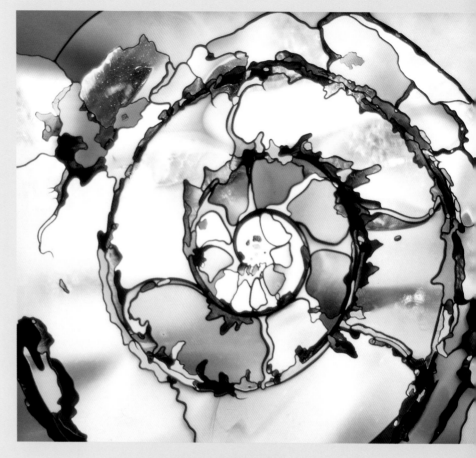

Rachel Schutt-Mesrahi
BACKLIT PANEL BEHIND ALTAR, JOHN MUIR HOSPITAL CHAPEL
(above and detail, opposite)
Life Unfolding
German blown glass, rondel pieces, copperfoiled and leaded
48" x 60" (122 cm x 152 cm)

9

Rachel Schutt-Mesrahi was first drawn to stained

glass by the material's ethereal qualities. She was

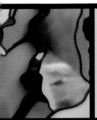

Rachel Schutt-Mesrahi

fascinated by the strong emotional response evoked

by the intensity of color and purity of light passing

through the glass. Beginning her career as a

craftsperson, Schutt-Mesrahi found herself intensely

inspired by the artistic process; thus, she made the

transition from craftsperson to stained glass artist.

Known for her eloquent execution, the artist

bases her pieces on subjects from uniquely personal

sources. Even though she has long admired the work

of artists such as Clifford Stills and Marcel Duchamp,

she relies on an internal muse. Schutt-Mesrahi puts

great faith in the universality of the experiences she

shares through her art. Personal and transgenerational

WINDOW IN PRIVATE COLLECTION
Static Movement
German blown glass, leaded and copperfoiled
30" x 70" (76 cm x 178 cm)

INDEPENDENT PANEL
Emerging Self (Self Portrait)
German blown glass, leaded and copperfoiled, copper foil overlays
36" x 24" (91 cm x 61 cm)

loss, the emotional balance between being an artist and being a mother, and the stories we all share in different ways serve as the subjects of, and inspiration for, her work.

More than anything else, though, Schutt-Mesrahi's work focuses on how we hide experiences and, more importantly, how we slowly reveal them to ourselves and each other. Thus, the cracks in her sidewalks crumble to reveal a new and different perspective behind. Dark colors melt into lighter hues, shading defines clarity, and a tentative balance between the obscured and the apparent are everywhere in Schutt-Mesrahi's creations.

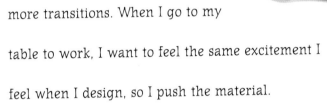

technique
Rachel Schutt-Mesrahi

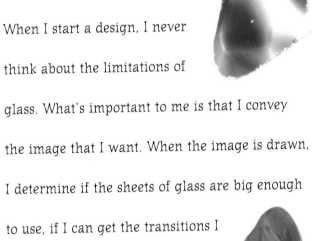

When I start a design, I never think about the limitations of glass. What's important to me is that I convey the image that I want. When the image is drawn, I determine if the sheets of glass are big enough to use, if I can get the transitions I want with the shapes I've drawn, and if I need more lines to convey

more transitions. When I go to my table to work, I want to feel the same excitement I feel when I design, so I push the material.

In seeking to test the limits, I often develop interesting techniques. A good example is the issue of line work. I want to run lead lines where they normally would not go. I manage to do this by cutting the heart out of the lead channel to run it right over a section of glass on either side of the panel.

The lead floats on the unbroken

surface and I lightly epoxy it to the glass.

Using this

method,

I can put a line almost anywhere

in the design.

When I am constructing my pieces, I feel like I am building something. I started out as a craftsperson because I loved working with my hands and the way the materials responded when I worked with them. After all these years, I still find myself as excited and challenged with this material as I was when I first started. I've never lost the love of working with leaded stained glass.

INDEPENDENT PANEL
Autumn Upheaval
German blown glass, etched
glass, leaded and copperfoiled
49" x 30" (124 cm x 76 cm)

INDEPENDENT PANEL
Circuitous Shadows
German blown glass, glass jewels, leaded,
copperfoiled with sheet lead overlays
3' x 3' (.9 m x .9 m)

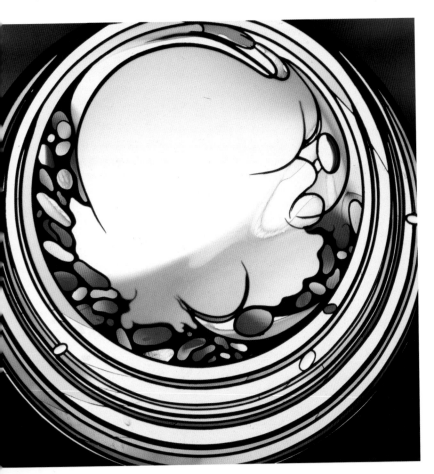

Rachel Schutt-Mesrahi

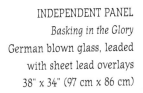

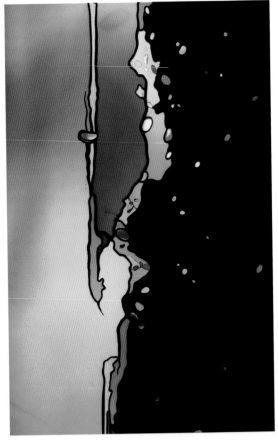

INDEPENDENT PANEL
Basking in the Glory
German blown glass, leaded
with sheet lead overlays
38" x 34" (97 cm x 86 cm)

DOUBLE DOORS
Movement Through Ethos
German and Fremont blown glasses, rondels
66" x 21" (168 cm x 53 cm)

WINDOW
Shadows Moving
German blown glass, glass jewels, leaded
21" x 55" (53 cm x 140 cm)

WINDOW, KENAN FLAGLER SCHOOL OF BUSINESS,
UNIVERSITY OF NORTH CAROLINA, CHAPEL HILL
A "Percent for Art" project. Project owned by North Carolina
Department of Cultural Resources.

David Wilson's charismatic commissions could easily stand alone as stunning works in glass. But viewing his art in isolation

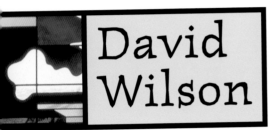

David Wilson

would defy the artist's greater purpose of establishing a partnership with the building and with its designer. Through his creations, Wilson gives due consideration to the sometimes unspoken exchange of ideas among the architect, those who use the space, and the artist. His constant awareness of the structural limitations of a particular space and the desires of his client serve to temper his considerable artistic skill.

Wilson's sensitivity to subject and user seems almost innate. His creative abilities, however, are the result of five years of rigorous fine-arts college education in his native England, culminating in postgraduate

work at the Central School of Arts and Crafts in London. There, he studied stained glass, mural painting, and sculpture. He would later spend more than a decade as a craftsman and designer for a prominent stained glass studio in New York City.

Leaving the studio environment behind, Wilson expanded on the geometric forms that had earlier captured his imagination. Geometry remains the starting point for his design process. He creates a linear image, adding color and form to that foundation. In a process he terms "reductionist," Wilson develops only the elements that seem fundamental to the nature of the piece. This stripping away of superfluous elements creates a more essential and powerful design that does not suffer from the artist's subtle use—or complete dismissal—of color.

WINDOW, KENAN FLAGLER SCHOOL OF BUSINESS (detail)

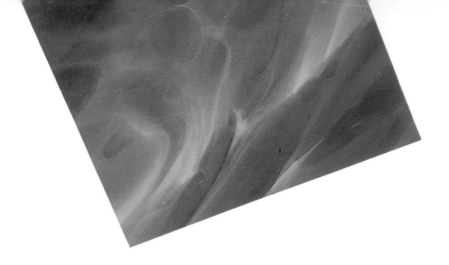

The first technical or visual aspect I consider is light. Light illuminating stained glass art—with the exception of artificially illuminated windows—is constantly changing. This is true not only through the day but also with the seasons.

The graphic quality of the lead line is yet another challenge. I find the lead line constantly intriguing.

Leaded glass has been incorporated in cathedrals in Europe since the Middle Ages, so you know that the technique works. Most of the work I have done is crafted in this traditional process, less often using brass, copper, or zinc channels as alternatives to lead. This does impose a certain aesthetic limitation, but it's a technical process with which I know I'm not going to have problems.

However, some architects find lead lines too busy. Consequently, one of the techniques I have been pursuing is treating

technique

David Wilson

larger sheets of structural glass with processes

other than the traditional ones. When you can

use sandblasting or special painted treatments on

larger surfaces, it opens up a new dimension in

the treatment of large, unbroken areas of glass.

Given the demands of my work and my

desire for large, unified planes, I am also investi-

gating sandwiching pieces of colored glass between

layers of structural glass without adhesives.

Ultimately, I want my work to incorporate

traditional and new techniques to take the union

of building and glass art one step further.

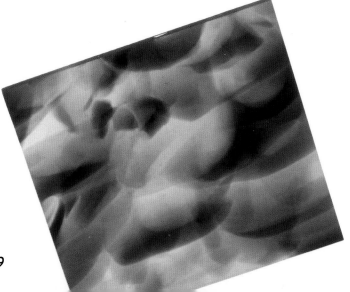

BARREL VAULT WINDOW,
ST. PAUL'S CATHOLIC CHURCH
Mouthblown transparent colors,
opalescents, and solar-tinted
window glass
20' x 16' (6.1 m x 4.9 m)

David Wilson

DOORS
Mouthblown transparent colors, opalescents,
dichroic glass, "spotted" glass, and clear bevels
7' x 18' (2.1 m x 5.5 m)

WINDOW
Mouthblown transparent colors, opalescents,
"spotted" colors, clear bevels
3' x 3' (.9 m x .9 m)

NEW JERUSALEM WINDOW,
CHRIST THE KING CATHOLIC CHURCH
Mouthblown antique transparent
colors, opalescents, and gold mirror
12' x 10' (3.7 m x 3 m)

WINDOW
Mouthblown antique transparent colors,
opalescents, and dichroic glass, copper channel
4' x 6' (1.2 m x 1.8 m)

Rick Melby's glass art light fixtures serve both as a testament to his talent and as a statement on

 the amazing versatility of the medium. Melby worked in a traditional glass studio for only a few years before striking out on his own to create work that trades the changing nuances of sunlight for those of a constant, artificial light source. In his light fixtures, Melby establishes an interplay between dynamic color and a sense of movement.

Melby's designs reflect varied influences, ranging from the line work of the art nouveau and art deco movements to the simple expression of seventeenth-century Japanese art. But one of the strongest influences on his artistic development was more thematic than stylistic. Melby found in the work of Marcel Duchamp a talent for presenting the mundane and everyday as new and interesting, an inclination that informs many of Melby's own pieces.

Like much of Duchamp's work, Melby's art is an exploration of context, of juxtaposing materials and concept in novel and thought-provoking ways. Melby focuses as much on how the art will be seen and perceived as on how it is executed. He hopes to lead the viewer to look beyond the obvious, to see how objects can be relevant on several levels, not all of which are connected to the work's original intent.

WALL SCONCE (opposite)
Cloud Light
Custom-made hand-cast opalescent glass,
etched glass fins, glass rod, copperfoiled
10" high x 12" wide x 5" deep (25 cm x 30 cm x 13 cm)

technique

Rick Melby

Much of my work utilizes techniques I learned in working with leaded glass. I simply applied these processes to three-dimensional forms. Over the years, I have picked up other techniques, including glass blowing, etching, and fusing.

I want my work to hold together over time, which is a challenge with light fixtures because of the heat problem. Even a modest bulb can generate a lot of heat, causing the copper foil that holds a piece together to come apart, or making the lamp too hot to touch, or even cracking the glass.

Consequently, I have to design a way for the heat to escape, but I also have to keep in mind the positioning of the light source. If I use a large piece of clear or fairly translucent colored glass, the bulb may create a visual hot spot that detracts

from the design. Although I sometimes use this hot

spot as a design element itself, I usually want to

eliminate it. After I've designed and built the piece,

I test it in my studio for quite some time before

delivering or installing it.

Of course, safety is the ultimate concern in

building and installing my work. I am very careful

because a badly wired lamp can cost people their

belongings, their home, and more. The

challenge is to create an artwork that safely

adds to the aesthetics of the environment

and serves the utilitarian purpose of

providing light.

TABLE-TOP LAMP
Las Olas
Hand-cast opalescent and machine-rolled glasses,
copperfoiled and leaded, painted wood base
14" high x 17" long x 4" wide (36 cm x 43 cm x 10 cm)

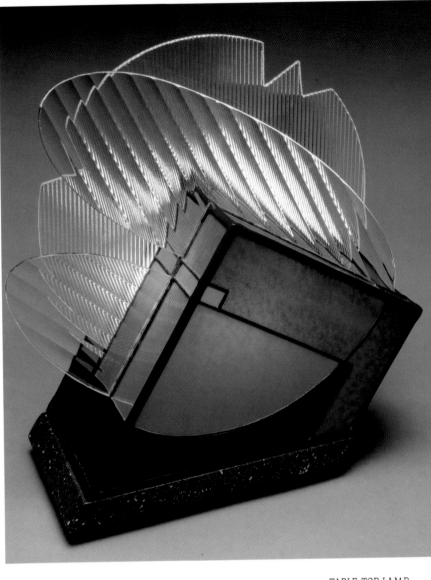

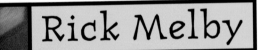

Rick Melby

TABLE-TOP LAMP
Orbit
Hand-cast opalescent and machine-rolled glasses,
copperfoiled and leaded, painted wood base
13" high x 13" long x 5" wide (33 cm x 33 cm x 13 cm)

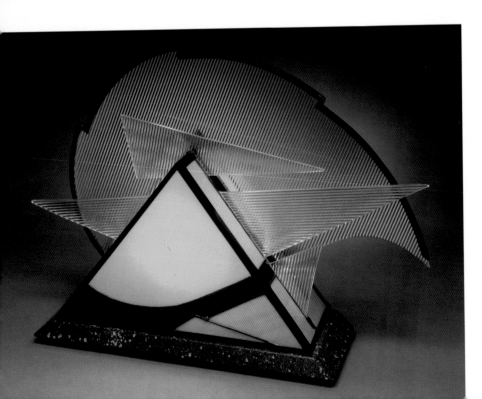

TABLE-TOP LAMP
Untitled
Opalescent and machine-rolled glasses,
copperfoiled and leaded, painted wood base
17" high x 12" long x 4" wide
(43 cm x 30 cm x 10 cm)

TABLE-TOP LAMP
Wing Thing
Hand-cast opalescent and etched machine-rolled
glasses, copperfoiled and leaded, painted wood base
12" high x 17" long x 4" wide (30 cm x 43 cm x 10 cm)

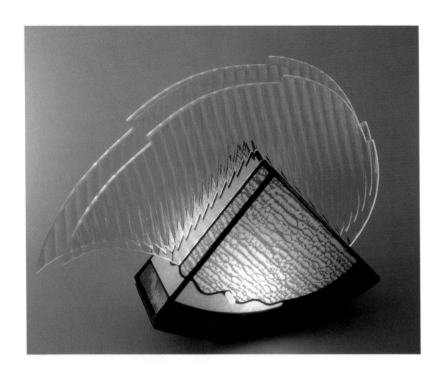

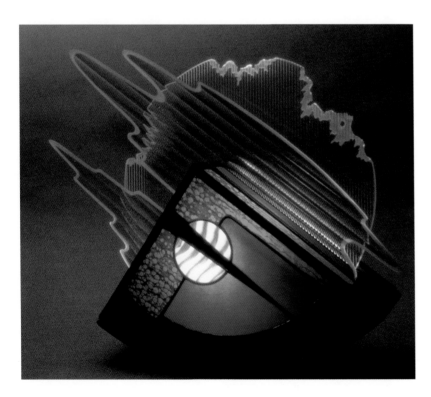

TABLE-TOP LAMP
Stratus
Hand-cast opalescent and etched machine-rolled glasses,
copperfoiled and leaded, painted wood base
13" high x 16" long x 5" wide (33 cm x 41 cm x 13 cm)

SCULPTURE
Scream
Etched plate glass, gold leaf, painted wood base
18" high x 11" long x 4" wide (46 cm x 28 cm x 10 cm)

Lutz Haufschild strives to reveal a building's soul with his architectural glass art. To him,

Lutz Haufschild

glass art has a lofty purpose and must endow the light entering the building with a significance that ultimately influences how the entire structure is perceived. He has pursued this goal for almost three decades, in small and large projects.

To create architectural art that meets these goals, Haufschild thinks beyond the material to the potential of the commission. He chose glass as a medium not because he fell in love with it, but because it allows him to work on an architectural scale that would be impossible in almost any other art form.

Haufschild does, however, consider in detail how an idea will translate into its material form. A project must expand his range and present new challenges that call for thoughtful solutions. The answer may lie in painting and etching a simple, vibrant design, such as *Blue Heart*, or in laminating bevels on plate glass, as with *Spectra Veil Sample*. His goal always remains the same: to continue a meaningful architectural artistic language that has a positive effect on the people who experience it.

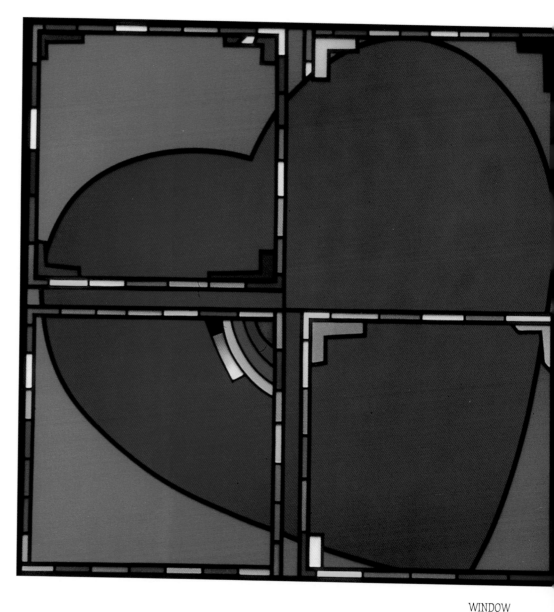

WINDOW
Blue Heart
Etched and painted glasses
30" x 30" (76 cm x 76 cm)

INTERIOR GLASS WALL (opposite)
Spectra Veil Sample
Layers of etched glass and painted
antique glasses, laminated
30" x 48" (76 cm x 122 cm)

technique

Lutz Haufschild

The desire to learn and to express myself in new ways has led me to experiment with new techniques and materials. For example, in trying to overcome the limitations of the lead line, I began to experiment with different laminating processes. In the commission *The Spectra Veil* for Toronto's Bata Shoe Museum, three layers of bevels and antique glass were laminated onto two layers of float glass. Although I used only clear glasses, by placing them in front of each other, an unusual opacity is achieved that fulfills the architectural requirements.

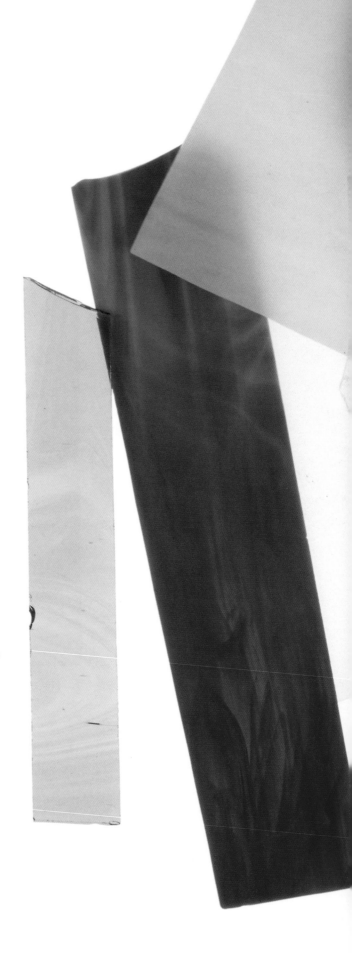

Because of this arrangement, the glass wall provides a new experience of the light itself.

I often work in large architectural formats. The complexity and size of my projects make it impossible to execute them myself. Since 1981 I have collaborated with three studios to fabricate my designs: Kits Glass Studios in Vancouver, Canada; Wilhelm Derix Glass Studios in Taunustein and Franz Meyer Studios in Munich, both in Germany. I work closely with the studios to ensure that my projects are completed true to the intent of the design, but I give them a lot of leeway because I like to benefit from their superior technical knowledge and experience.

Lutz Haufschild

BACKLIT INSTALLATION FOR STADIUM ENTRANCE
(detail showing Pete Rose)
Tribute to Baseball
Cast glass, total piece
60' x 16' (18.3 m x 4.9 m)

WINDOW IN CIVIC CENTER
The Fire Fighting Window
Layers of etched and painted antique glasses, laminated
8.5' x 16' (2.6 m x 4.9 m)

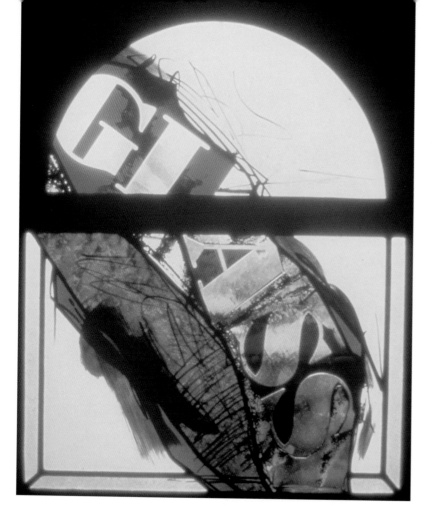

WINDOW, MUSEUM OF CONTEMPORARY GLASS
Gl/ass
Etched and painted stained glasses
48" x 36" (122 cm x 91 cm)

INTERIOR GLASS WALL, CORPORATE HEADQUARTERS
Time and Space
Etched and painted glasses
8.5' x 8' (2.6 m x 2.4 m)

ONE OF FOUR CHURCH WINDOWS (WINTER)
The Four Seasons
Etched and painted antique glasses
32' x 6' (9.8 m x 1.8 m)

Kuni Kajiwara first became fascinated with the potential of stained glass as an art student in Kobe, Japan. Her

Kuni Kajiwara

initial interest was heightened during her studies of graphic design in London. To Kajiwara, the stained glass windows in many of the older European buildings seemed almost three-dimensional in their vibrancy. She was transfixed by the metamorphosis of light into color and decided to pursue her own vision in this brilliant art form.

From the start, Kajiwara's exploration has gone in two design directions. In one aspect of her work, she creates a contemporary look, using a detailed and elaborate geometric vocabulary with subtle complementary colors. This work—exemplified by the skylight she created for the Hotel Taishoya—is precise, clean, and balanced.

In contrast, Kajiwara also crafts richly colored abstract pieces. She often works with *dalle de verre*, known as slab glass, to create dense, primitive pieces that reflect more pure emotion than exacting glass cuts. This work reflects the gentle, understated nature of an older Japan, the Japan of calligraphy, Shinto temples, and Zen gardens.

The two sides of Kajiwara's style find equal voice in her commissions. She doesn't feel she has to choose between the two, because each has different strengths and only one will be appropriate in a given space. The result is an ideal match of artwork to space.

SKYLIGHT, HOTEL TAISHOYA
Untitled
Handblown stained glass, painted glass
16.4' x 16.6' (5 m x 5.1 m)

I live in a remote area of Japan that is very beautiful and informs most of my design efforts, even when they are geometric in style. I can sit and look out over rice fields and mountains, which give me a lot of inspiration for sketching. I find sketching is a great exercise and really frees my creativity before I have to take on the technical considerations inherent in fabricating my pieces. All of my lines and colors come from the sketchbook first and foremost.

The commission I am working on usually determines my design style that, in turn, determines what the technical considerations will be. My geometric compositions may be more complex than my abstract designs, but they are usually easier to design because the linear nature of the piece makes it easier to include structural reinforcement. I find that geometric designs work better for large or difficult installations, such as skylights.

technique
Kuni Kajiwara

When working with abstract designs, I often like to work with *dalle de verre. Dalle de verre* comes in foot-long slabs that I cut with a chisel to create the pieces for my design. The beauty of this glass is that it is more than an inch thick, which makes the color very saturated, very dark and dramatic. My two different styles offer different technical and aesthetic challenges and, using both, they always seem fresh to me.

WINDOW
Banksia
Stained glass, etched and painted, with appliqué
28" (71 cm) in diameter

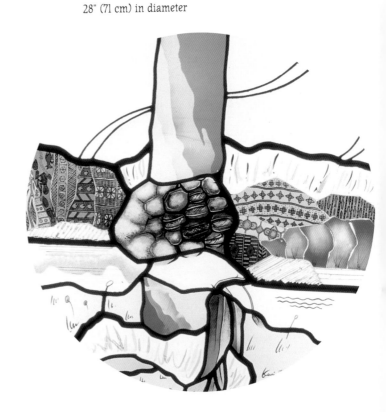

WINDOW, SAISEIKAI HOSPITAL
The Life
Dalle de verre, in epoxy and sand frame
7' x 8' x 4" (2.1 m x 2.4 m x 10 cm)

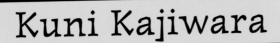

Kuni Kajiwara

WINDOW
Parnassius
Laminated stained glass, painted and sandblasted
30" (76 cm) in diameter

SKYLIGHT
Mandrara
Laminated stained glass, etched, painted, and sandblasted
6' x 4" x 8' (1.8 m x 10 cm x 2.4 m)

WINDOW, FUJI CITY LIBRARY
Untitled
Dalle de verre
12' x 3' x 3" (3.7 m x .9 m x 8 cm)

Sigrídur Asgeirsdóttir breaks the rules. This

innovative Icelandic glass artist challenges the

Sigrídur Asgeirsdóttir

very convention that, on the face of things, makes

glass art distinctive: its transparency. She uses

dense glass colors and dark reflective paints to

focus interest on the design, the positioning of

the pieces, and the play of shadows and light on

edges and surfaces.

Asgeirsdóttir has long created intense designs

in glass. Her recent exhibition pieces undermine

all assumptions viewers may have about glass.

In panels alive with one or two energetic colors,

she crafts a language of hard-edged angles and

violent splashes of glass paint. Using repetitive

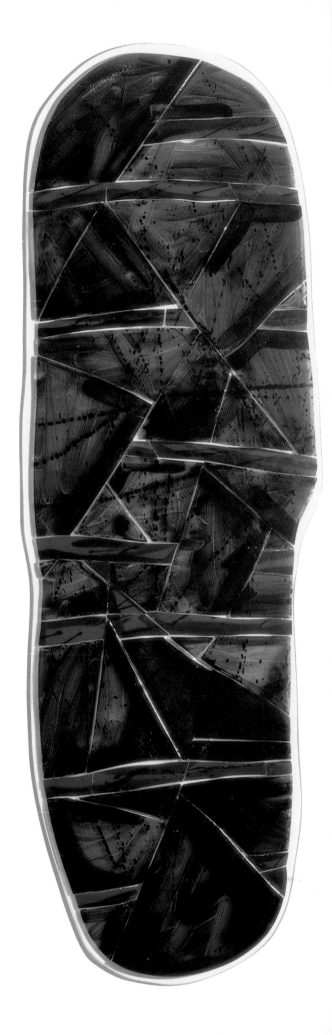

EXHIBITION PIECE
Genesis
Laminated stained glass on clear glass, thick painting
59" x 23.5" (150 cm x 60 cm)

and juxtaposed panels, Asgeirsdóttir establishes an entirely different way of viewing the material.

Art critics and peers have commented that this drama of contrasts and forceful presentation echoes the harshness and beauty of Asgeirsdóttir's homeland. But this interpretation discounts the originality of her inspiration and creativity. She was first drawn to glass because of its contradictions—the tension in the material between its fragility and its forcefulness—and its power to transform. Asgeirsdóttir has taken that fascination a giant leap forward to a place where the viewer must leave preconceived ideas at the door and expect only the unexpected.

WINDOW
Gardar & Nattfari
Stained and clear textured glasses
29.5' x 29.5' (9 m x 9 m)

technique

Sigrídur Asgeirsdóttir

Because I was taught well, technical and structural demands are always in the back of my mind. But I do play with them in my sculptural works.

I often float very big pieces on a wall without any visible means of support, or I may lean a piece against a wall looking slightly out of balance. I think this generally goes unnoticed by nonexpert viewers, but those familiar with the weight of glass will be pleasantly surprised.

Technically, these pieces are great fun to create. The heavy glass base has to be cut and drilled by an outside vendor, while at the studio we are cutting the image, cleaning it, and lining it up for the paint. When the glass is ready to be

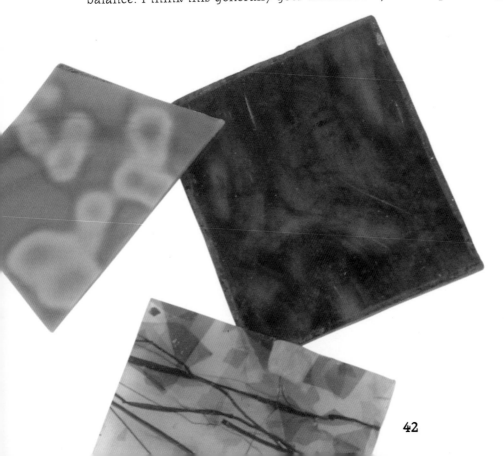

painted, the studio goes quiet and the air is filled with tension. Painting on glass for me is a very physical thing—the smell, the loading of the brush, the immediate impact of the paint to the glass. It is like a never-ending love affair. I still cut glass when I have to, but I rather think of myself as a conductor making sure that the emotion and thought get transferred from the sketch to the finished piece. I have no need to be all the instruments, only to know that they are working together.

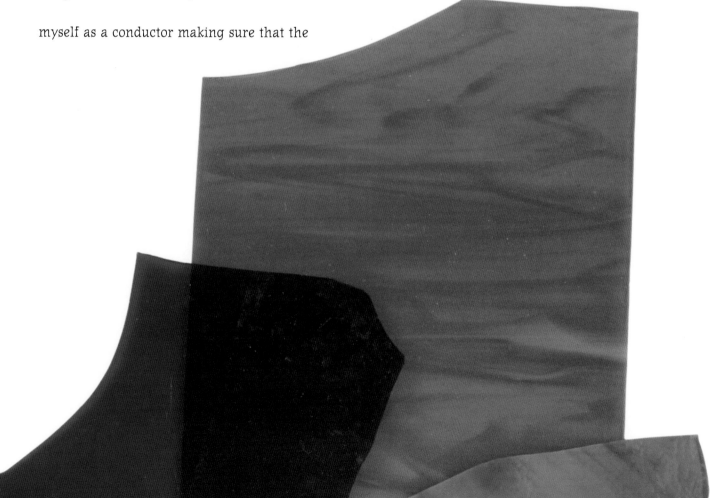

Sigrídur Asgeirsdóttir

EXHIBITION PIECE
Triangles
Stained glass, painted and laminated on clear glass
39.5" x 98.5" (100 cm x 250 cm)

EXHIBITION PIECE
Six Moments in Time
Stained glass, painted and
laminated on clear glass
90.5" x 6" (230 cm x 15 cm) each piece

EXHIBITION PIECE
The Silence of the Sea
Stained glass, painted and laminated on clear glass
59" x 71" (150 cm x 180 cm)

INDEPENDENTLY HUNG PANEL
Untitled
Stained and clear glasses, painted
19.5" x 19.5" (50 cm x 50 cm)

INTERIOR WINDOW,
CORPORATE BUILDING
Night
Stained glass
39.5' x 9.75' (12 m x 3 m)

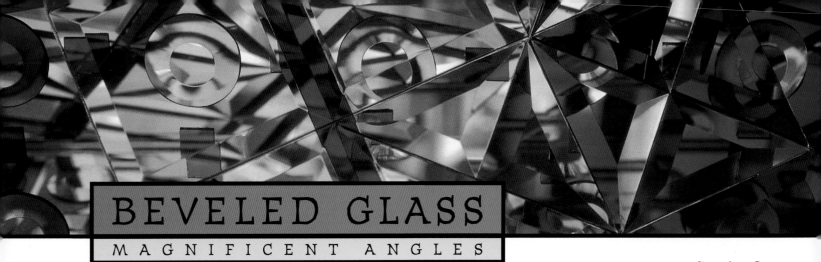

BEVELED GLASS
MAGNIFICENT ANGLES

Kenneth vonRoenn
GLASS COLUMNS
UNIVERSITY OF TOLEDO
(detail, above)

It has been said that diamonds fall second to the crisp, linear brilliance and charismatic glitter of beveled glass. An exaggeration, perhaps, but not by much. Beveled clear glass acts as a prism, splitting transmitted light into a transient rainbow of sparkling hues. Because of this property, the technique continues to gain popularity among contemporary glass artists.

Larry Zgoda uses custom-beveled jewels as thematic threads running through his timeless architectural panels. His designs complement the spaces they occupy, adding vivid focal points without overpowering other elements of the architecture. Shelley Jurs prefers to exploit negative and positive spaces within her panels, creating works that rely more on eloquence of lines and opposing forms than on the impact of strong colors.

Virginia Hoffman plays with the perception of bevels as fairly orderly pieces of glass. She creates fluid, abstract glass art, designing the bevels in odd, irregular shapes that bend and curve to the needs of the design. In contrast, the talented architectural stained glass artist Kenneth vonRoenn has increasingly worked with straight-line rectangular bevels. His linear designs offer textural interest that intensifies the innate sensual appeal and tactile allure of the glass.

Finally, Carl Powell uses innovative beveling techniques to bring his panels to life. He bevels both sides of the glass and uses other tricks of the trade to create designs full of active optical and geometric illusions.

Kenneth vonRoenn
WINDOW
Untitled
Beveled squares and rectangles, stained glass
2' x 4.9' (.6 m x 1.5 m)

Larry Zgoda's appreciation of stained glass as an architectural art form began almost three

Larry Zgoda

decades ago, when he spent much of his free time

photographing prewar buildings in Chicago. He developed an admiration for the elegant ornamentation—especially the stained glass—that was so much a part of the charm of those older buildings.

His fascination led him to a basic course in stained glass. He quickly expanded on this foundation, learning from other craftsmen, books, and trial and error. Taking a job with a dealer of architectural ornamentation, Zgoda spent two years rebuilding vintage stained glass panels and re-creating old styles in new panels. He eventually opened his own studio and began developing his own unique style in glass.

INTERIOR WINDOW BETWEEN TWO ROOMS
Beveled ruby jewels, black and red stained glasses, beveled machined glass
16" x 34" (41 cm x 86 cm)

Zgoda's art focuses on the relationship of the glass design to its architectural context. To this end, he uses color sparingly, allowing large sections of clear glass to act as a foil for smaller pieces of subdued color. This sensitive balancing of color and light results in panels that complement the architecture. Unusual beveled pieces attract the viewer's eye and entice further exploration of architectural forms and colors.

The essence of Zgoda's talent lies in his ability to cut away clutter and still maintain enough complexity and interaction of geometric form to create intense visual interest. He uses this ability in pursuit of his ongoing goal to help revive the lost spirit of architectural art.

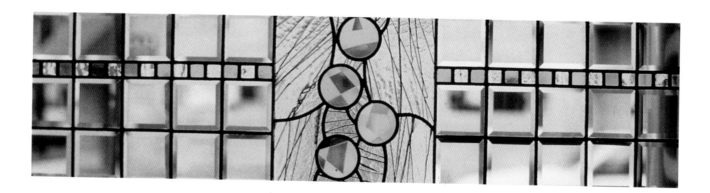

WINDOW
Beveled optical lenses with random facets,
Asahi opal glass, antique clear glass
36" x 12" (91 cm x 30 cm)

technique

Larry Zgoda

I design panels to be compatible with the buildings they occupy. I also consider how the design form will work with the physical structure of the panel, because the piece needs to withstand whatever may come along. The structure needs to be strong enough to be there a hundred years from now, and I want the design to be as appropriate then as when I first created it.

My designs are affected foremost by available light. I work with subtle colors, and clear and white glasses. The light affects where and how I place different types and colors of glass, and I often take samples to the site to see how they will catch the light. I incorporate bevels to bend the view through the panel and to alter the light coming through the panel.

In constructing a panel, I like to be conservative. I create the initial sketch by putting in the reinforcing bar lines, constructing the lead

lines of the design afterward. I use a flat reinforcing bar, so that the width is no greater than that of the lead lines in the window. I like to establish a foundation of very predictable geometry, usually on the lower portion of a window, and then let go with a wilder design on the upper portion. This predictable base is a way for me to work in structural considerations, while providing a visual anchor to the panel. It also allows me to use large unbroken panes of fairly nondescript glass to contrast with smaller, colored beveled pieces. This contrast is key to my designs; it makes the colors and planes of the beveled pieces come alive.

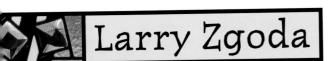

Larry Zgoda

WINDOW
Beveled clear glass, custom-beveled
wire-glass squares and circles
30" x 14" (76 cm x 36 cm)

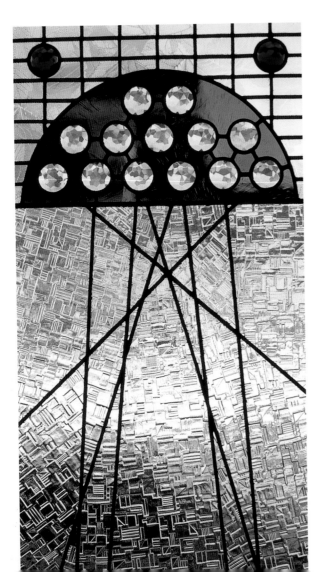

WINDOW
Blue glass oval inset with
antique beveled jewels,
machined glass, cut pink jewels
16" x 30" (41 cm x 76 cm)

WINDOW
Austrian crystal jewels cut and faceted into triangles,
beveled wire-glass squares, clear glass
24" x 66" (61 cm x 168 cm)

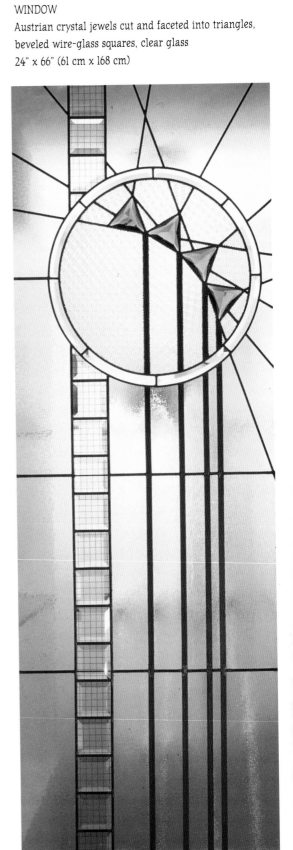

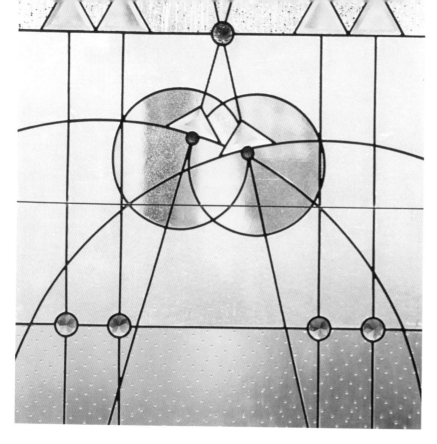

CASEMENT WINDOW
Asahi blue-opal beveled jewels, beveled triangles,
ruby faceted jewels, stained glass, machined glass
31" x 33" (79 cm x 84 cm)

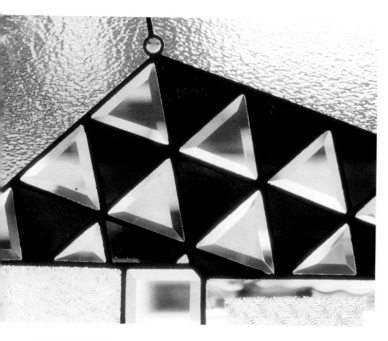

AUTONOMOUS PANEL (detail)
Beveled clear glass triangles, cut gold-pink jewels, custom-beveled
peach plate, beveled on opposite sides (cube)
14" x 16" (36 cm x 41 cm)

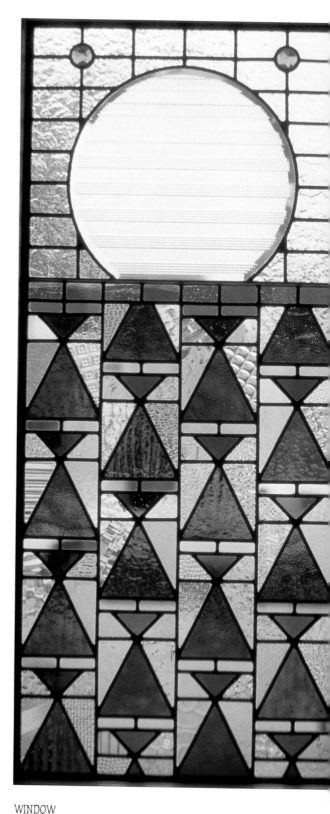

WINDOW
Christmas
Beveled, textured glass circle, gold antique jewels, gold
antique glass, gold ruby-stained glass, hand rolled clear glass
16" x 36" (41 cm x 91 cm)

53

The pursuit of glass as art and career was a

logical evolution for Shelley Jurs, marking the

Shelley Jurs

culmination of

an interest in

hands-on arts

and crafts

dating from childhood. She was an art major in

college, eventually transferring to the renown

California College of Arts and Crafts. Focusing

on ceramics, Jurs explored a range of other media

as well. An invitation from her brother-in-law to

spend the summer working at his glass studio

marked a turning point. As a result, she left

school to work in the studio full-time.

Two years later, seeking to explore and

expand upon her own glass design sensibilities,

Jurs attended the Swansea College of Art in

South Wales. She then became a personal

assistant to legendary German glass artist

DESIGN SERIES DOOR
Handblown textured and clear glasses, hand-cast jewels
3' x 6.8' (.9 m x 2.1 m)

Ludwig Shaffrath, an essential influence on the development of Jurs's own style in glass. Shaffrath taught her the importance of using the line as a defining graphic element.

Jurs emphasizes her line work through the clean angles of the cast beveled pieces she so often uses. She intentionally avoids bold splashes of color, opting instead for the soothing and meditative elegance of neutral colors and clear and textured glasses. Her goal is to create an uplifting space for the viewers of the work; light and its transition through the glass are key principle concerns in achieving that goal.

DOOR
Diamond Heights
Handblown glass, cast jewels, in steel frame
3' x 8' (.9 m x 2.4 m)

Bevels and glass jewels have become a trademark of my work for many reasons. I enjoy how the repetition of simple geometric modules creates new, expanded forms of expression, and I prize the illusion of depth and layered light that beveled glass offers. In addition, the creation of color through the use of no color—taking advantage of the prismatic qualities of the bevel—reminds me of some mystical life force.

In taking advantage of this potential, I have become more and more involved with integrating structure. Structure and design can be unified to create a wonderful style. As with wood, steel, aluminum, and lead came, or other framing components that join and contain the glass pieces, essential structural elements must become integral parts of the design. In contemplating a design, I may engage an engineer or other specialist to ensure these issues

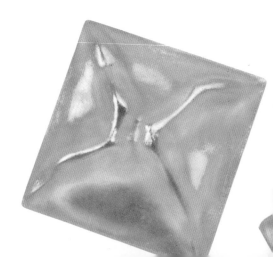

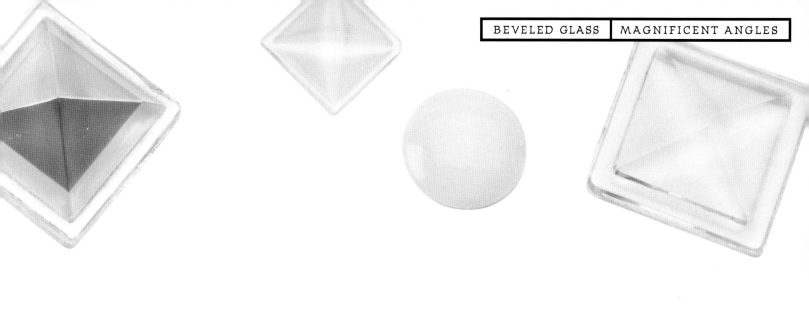

are being dealt with so that the piece functions

structurally. That's simply part of my design

process. This is in keeping with a basic technical

philosophy of creating works to last. I don't

believe in pushing materials beyond their innate

ability merely for the benefit of some tricky

technique that eventually causes the physical

breakdown of the original expres-

sion. There must always be a

marriage between materials

and design, one that endures

through time.

Shelley Jurs

MOUNTED DOOR
Ninelite
Handblown glass and hand-cast glass jewels
32" x 6.8' (81 cm x 2.1 m)

DOUBLE DOORS
Handblown and hand-cast glass jewels, bevels
6' x 8' (1.8 m x 2.4 m)

BATHROOM WINDOWS (opposite)
Radiant Light
Handblown glass and cast beveled jewels
6' x 8' (1.8 m x 2.4 m)

DOME SKYLIGHT
Celestial Phenomena
Handblown seedy and reamy glasses
and hand-cast jewels, bevels
22' (6.7 m) in diameter

DOUBLE DOORS
Black lacquer frame, beveled and round
jewels, clear and textured glasses
5' x 7' (1.5 m x 2.1 m)

Kenneth vonRoenn

Kenneth vonRoenn's training as an architect gives him a unique perspective on the potential of, and unique consider-ations inherent in, glass art. In 1991, he purchased the studio where he began his glass art career, giving him the control to select commissions that focus on considerations of interest to him, such as the way light entering a space affects the occupants of that space.

VonRoenn's experience gives him an insider's understanding of how a glass design relates to the larger environment. In creating a panel, he considers how the space will be used, how often—and for how long—the viewer will be exposed to the piece, and what overall tone the architecture sets. He focuses on completing the architecture, making it more memorable, exciting, and interesting than it would be without the glass art.

60

Over the last decade, vonRoenn has increasingly used bevels in his pieces. Beyond the prismatic effects such elements provide, he is attracted to the ability of bevels to fracture the image as seen through the panel, creating an impressionistic sense. He uses bevels to elevate the sense of color and the character of the light, making the inanimate articulate and adding expression to the environment. VonRoenn's work adds an intellectual lyricism to the static combination of building materials. It provides thoughtful poetry in glass, food as much for the soul and mind as for the eye.

GLASS COLUMNS, UNIVERSITY OF TOLEDO
(detail showing the complexity and chaos
of the overlaid forms)

GLASS COLUMNS,
UNIVERSITY OF TOLEDO (opposite)
Layers of beveled clear and stained glasses create a form
that becomes less understandable the closer the viewer gets.
10' x 24" (3 m x 61 cm)

technique

Kenneth vonRoenn

Structure is as critical as aesthetics within architectural art. I try to solve the fundamental issues of structure relatively early in design development. These initial structural considerations do not in any way lessen my enthusiasm for the project. In fact, I find that the exploration of structure—the eventual construction of the work of art—informs my aesthetics.

In the initial stages of creating the design, I look at the options and choose the best possible structural choices for the panel on which I'm working. I take into account the panel's exposure, its size, and its environment— where it will be placed. I keep the concerns in mind right through to actual fabrication.

I work closely with my studio of craftspeople to develop techniques for the specific structural challenges of my work. An example is a reinforcing system that we've come to rely on. The system deals with the inherent forces on a glass panel—the perpendicular force of wind load, perhaps the weight of a moving panel within a door, and the secondary force of gravity. We organize our reinforcing bars to counteract those forces by positioning bars horizontally on one surface and vertically on another, and anchoring them securely to the frame. By developing solutions specific to each of my projects, my art, like the buildings in which it is situated, will stand the test of time.

Kenneth vonRoenn

DOORS
Straight-line bevels laminated end-to-end,
stained glass, textured glass
2'1"x 6'8" (.6 m x 2.1 m)
each door

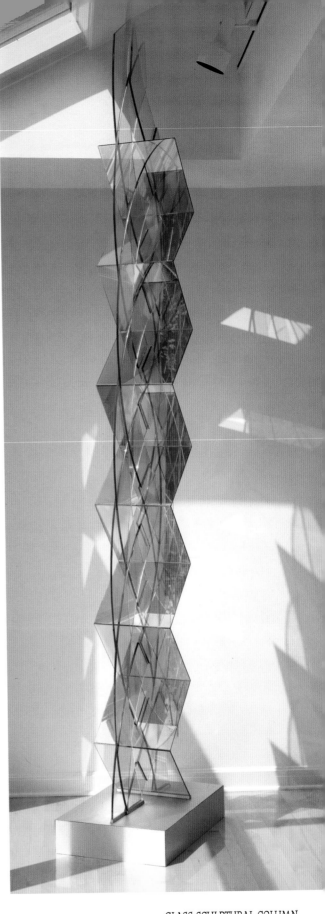

GLASS SCULPTURAL COLUMN
Stained and clear glasses
12' x 12" x 12" (3.7 m x 30 cm x 30 cm)

ENTRYWAY
Straight-line bevels, round glass
jewels, stained glass, clear glass
8' x 8' (2.4 m x 2.4 m)

Carl Powell

Carl Powell considers the limitations of the medium of glass art as challenges to his talent. He refuses to let the traditional or the accepted way of doing things confine his vision. His background as a painter drives him to create unusual and original optical effects rarely found in glass art. Twenty-five years ago, as a student of painting, he came across photographs of the stunning stained glass work of the painter Joseph Albers. That discovery led him to take a summer job in a stained glass studio.

Powell explored beveling as an opportunity to create a new interplay of shapes and textures. Crafted in colorless glass, his beveled pieces started as a way to escape the confines of studio commissions, where clients wanted pieces to include every color of the rainbow. After Powell moved to California, a client asked him to create a piece in his signature style, but including some

color. He reintroduced color on his own terms, using bold but limited splashes of vibrant hues against large fields of clear and textured glasses.

Powell's unconventional style combines beveled polygons, cylinders, and cubes with shadowy textured glass and vibrant shocks of color. His innovative approach to his art does not stop with his style. He often creates works in multiple panels that the client can rearrange to suit his or her personal preference. But true to their nature, his works never lose the balance of chaos and control that is so much their hallmark.

WINDOW (opposite)
Carnival
Pale blue and white creamy antique handblown German glasses, beveled shapes including cylinders, discs, and cubes
10' x 6' (3 m x 1.8 m)

PENTHOUSE WINDOW (detail, above)
Untitled
Clear background glass textured to provide privacy, stained glass, machined glass, beveled shapes
17' x 2' (5.2 m x .6 m) total window

technique

Carl Powell

I began beveling as a way to depart from the traditional confines of stained glass design, and the techniques I use evolved from there. After a while, it was important to me to be able to do something different, without being told how it had to be done.

I became interested in the shapes you can create by beveling on both sides, causing them to appear much thicker than they really are, like optical illusions. I like to take long pieces of thick glass and just multifacet the whole surface. Then, when you walk in front of the finished piece, it really becomes kinetic, capturing colors from the outside environment and making them dance across the surface of the glass. Another technique I use to create a drawing effect is overleading, where I run lead right over the glass and just stop it, without going to another piece of lead.

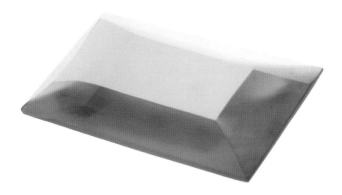

These techniques are ways to expand my glass

vocabulary. I think the artist has to continually

search for new ways to express meaning in his or

her work. The flexibility I've found in beveling

allows me that exploration, in much

the same way that a painter

uses his paints.

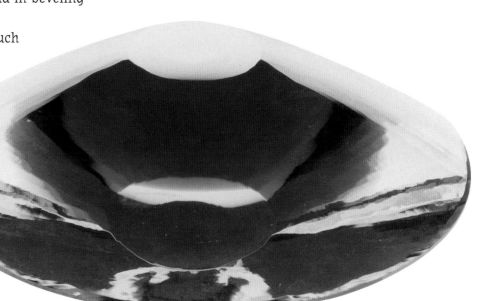

Carl Powell

FREESTANDING SCREEN
Navigator
Variety of textured and clear glasses,
stained glass, and beveled shapes
7' x 5.5' (2.1 m x 1.7 m)

Navigator (detail)
This portion of the screen shows the optical illusions created by beveling
on both sides of a piece of glass. The heart is a fully beveled piece that
broke and was then cut, beveled, rejoined, and leaded into the screen.

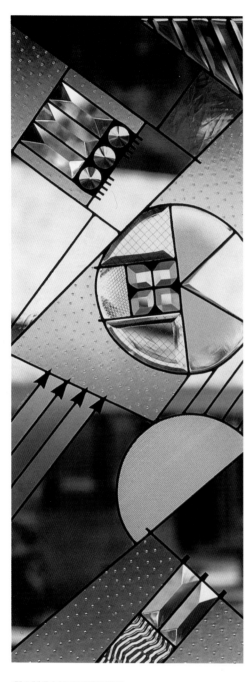

GLASS DOOR ENTRYWAY
Untitled
Beveled 1.25" (3.5 cm) glass to create a prismatic
effect, and arrows created by overlaying lead on
the glass
6' x 2.5' (1.8 m x .8 m)

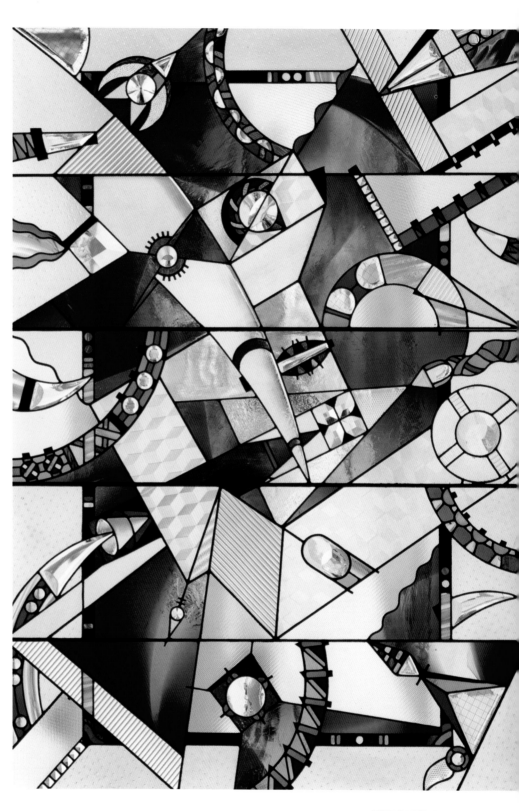

FIVE-PANEL WINDOW
Flamenco in Cobalt
Variegated cobalt German handblown glass, extensive
beveling throughout, steel frame around each section
11' x 8' (3.4 m x 2.4 m)

Virginia Hoffman's design skills were well developed by the time she found her way into

the world of glass art.

Shortly after graduating from college with a degree in graphic design, she veered off her career path in advertising to take a job at a local stained glass studio. Her design skills and talents, honed in the two-dimensional world of paper, were vividly translated into seductive three-dimensional form.

Drawing on her eclectic interests that range from mid-century abstract expressionists to the German Bauhaus movement and beyond, Hoffman has created a fluid yet dynamic style that seems to transcend the material in which she works. Most of the bevels she uses are custom shaped to her specifications. These

ENTRYWAY DOORS
(detail showing the curved and pyramid peak bevels and textured background glasses)

oddly shaped, curved pieces offer the allure of a facet without interrupting the flow of the design.

Hoffman uses her bevels to their best advantage, accentuating their sharp clarity with complementary clear and textured glasses. She limits her use of colors, rarely incorporating more than one in any given piece. In Hoffman's work, the simplicity of sound design transcends the complexity of a crowded palette.

DOUBLE PANELS FOR ENTRYWAY
Reamy clear glass, crackle glass, pink-gold stained glass
45" x 65" (114 cm x 165 cm)

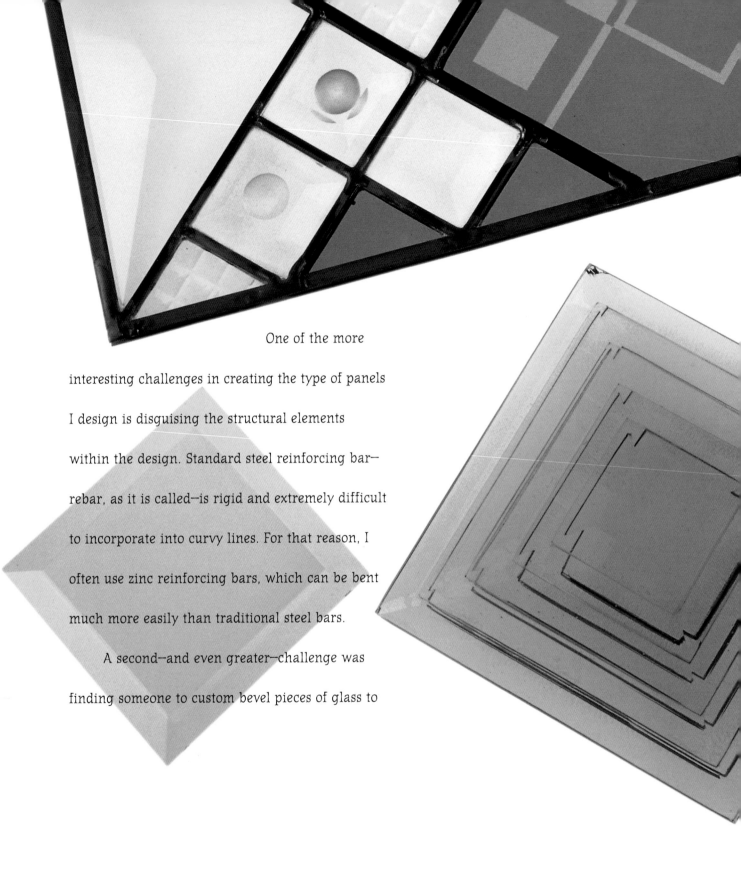

One of the more interesting challenges in creating the type of panels I design is disguising the structural elements within the design. Standard steel reinforcing bar—rebar, as it is called—is rigid and extremely difficult to incorporate into curvy lines. For that reason, I often use zinc reinforcing bars, which can be bent much more easily than traditional steel bars.

A second—and even greater—challenge was finding someone to custom bevel pieces of glass to

technique
Virginia Hoffman

my specifications. My work is abstract and fluid, and I usually don't want to use straight, mass-produced bevels. Putting a facet on an uneven or oddly shaped piece of glass is no easy task. I was lucky enough to find a master beveler named Dan Woodward in Portland, Oregon. We have worked together quite well, and Dan has been able to execute bevels to the most difficult specifications I can imagine.

Many times, I draw a design and actually place the peak of the bevel so that it complements the lines in the design. This sort of visual interest is key to what I do. Having a relationship with a beveler who is able to do that type of exacting work greatly expands the possibilities of using bevels in my work.

Virginia Hoffman

WINDOW
German handblown glass, straight-line stock bevels, beveled pyramids
58" x 63" (147 cm x 160 cm)

DOUBLE DOORS AND ARCH-TOP WINDOW
Desag antique thick glass used for bevels, stained glass,
reamy used in background glass
6' x 15' (1.8 m x 4.6 m)

STAINED GLASS WALL, CORPORATE BUILDING
Flemish Pilkington clear textured glass,
Fremont stained glass, and beveled circles
8' x 11' (2.4 m x 3.4 m)

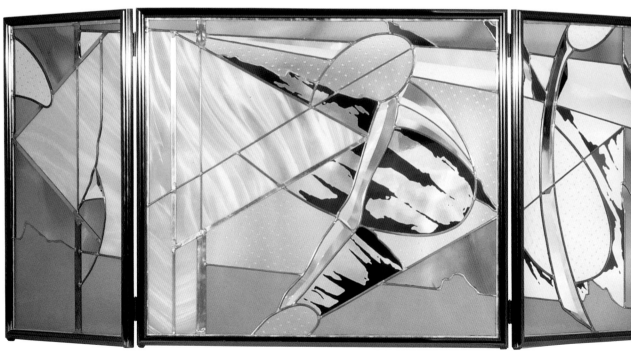

FIREPLACE SCREEN
Beveled thick glass, blue
acid-etched glass,
machined glass
45" x 65" (114 cm x 165 cm)
(detail, above, showing
the extremely difficult
beveled curved pieces
and the acid-etched
blue glass)

PAINTED GLASS
FRAGILE BRUSHSTROKES

Painting on stained glass is an adventure in the modulation of light and color unlike any other medium. The artist controls the translucency of color and line and can, if they so choose, escape the traditional confines of the lead line by painting on an unbroken panel of glass, or by crossing the lead line with the painting itself. Traditionally done by laying down a thick matte of paint and cutting form out of that, modern glass painters have adapted materials and techniques to suit their own styles and to create works amazingly original in conception and execution.

Serving as a bridge between old and new in both techniques and style, master glass painter Patrick Reyntiens executes designs combining an amazingly refined eye for color with unparalleled wit and insight. His philosophical approach and dynamic style have inspired numerous artists, including Ellen Mandelbaum. Mandelbaum has long since followed her own muse to develop a boldly distinctive style. She creates beautiful panels with organic and free-flowing forms.

Linda Lichtman
INDEPENDENT PANEL (detail, above)
Inside the Outside
Vitreous paint, acid-etched,
stained, and leaded glasses
11" x 16" (28 cm x 41 cm)

Linda Lichtman has chosen a more colorful and often figural style. Her whimsical and upbeat representations contrast starkly with her darkly dramatic colors. British painter Debora Coombs shares this sense of color. She explores the universal themes of the human condition with striking sensitivity all the more amazing given her mathematical predilections.

Marie Foucault's wild and uninhibited brushwork illuminates the stories and personal revelations that take form on all of her panels. Mary Mackey also allows her brush free rein as she finds her style moving away from the figural and into a more expressionistic realm.

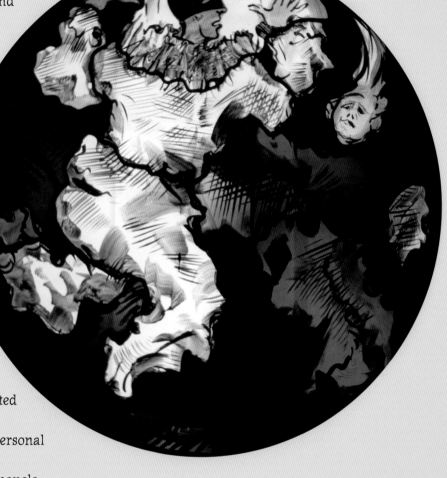

Patrick Reyntiens
ONE OF EIGHT INDEPENDENT "CIRCUS" RONDELS
Clown Piece
German, French, and English antique glasses,
painted *alla prima* using matte and rapid brushstrokes
29" (74 cm) in diameter

Patrick Reyntiens

Master glass painter Patrick Reyntiens has inspired and educated generations of stained

glass artists. He has been essential in helping to expand the range and vocabulary of the art in both Europe and America. His book, *The Technique of Stained Glass*, is considered the seminal text on the art. Reyntiens's myriad accomplishments include extensive writings on a range of subjects and commissions throughout Europe and America. But as impressive as this resume might be, it falls second to his refined skill as a painter and glass artist, exhibited in his unerring control of color and light.

That use of color is the first element the viewer notices. Even to the untrained eye, a panel

WINDOW (detail)
Twelve Heads of Dame Edna
German, French, and antique glasses
55" x 29" (140 cm x 74 cm)

painted by Reyntiens is a visual feast—luscious, enigmatic, and satisfying. He works in a vivid spectrum of related colors, balancing intensity, value, and hue so that the entire work is unified. In *Hommage à Fauré*, a cornucopia of colors mesh in such a vibrant, charismatic image that it seems contradictory to call the work a still life.

This animation characterizes Reyntiens's work, from figurative pieces that call to mind the masterpieces of medieval times to the witty and sparkling images of a more contemporary bent. His purposeful and confident use of color, and the synthesis of that color with lines of paint and lead, remain unmatched among glass painters.

INDEPENDENT PANEL
Hommage à Fauré
German, French, and antique glasses
39" x 28" (99 cm x 71 cm)

I'm not a technical wizard, as such. Expression and artistic intent must take precedence over mere technical cleverness. If you do a thing, from riding a bicycle to going to the moon, you must find the right way of doing it.

A major challenge early on was the Baptistery Window at Coventry Cathedral. I had to do an enormous John Piper watercolor in glass. It was 82 feet high by 55 feet wide (25 meters high by 16.8 meters wide), presenting an unusual first "trial by fire." The top of the window was to be different blues that needed to have a common element when lit. I discovered in London a source of "railroad" glass, a turquoise blue mechanical

glass of uniform color. I plated the glass to the window and laid down the varied blues of the design on top of it. The railroad glass acted as a subtle unifying tone, yet it was not discernible to the eye.

Glass painters in particular need to play with transparency versus translucency. I've always worked in glass as a painter, rather than as a craftsman, and my glass expression depends on the exploration between translucency and transparency. I think you need to move quickly and assertively, which is why I have always painted very fast. I believe it is the only way to make a piece have sparkle, verve, and a life of its own.

Patrick Reyntiens

WINDOW IN MACAULEY HOUSE APSE, ENGLAND
Commercial factory glass, German antique glass,
alla prima painting, slumping
11' x 16.5' (3.4 m x 5 m)

ONE OF TWELVE WINDOWS
The Last Labor of Hercules
German, French, and English antique glasses
16.5" x 15" (42 cm x 38 cm)

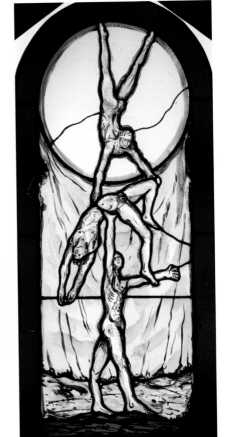

INDEPENDENT PANEL
Homage to the Olympiads
Alla prima painting (some pieces of
glass are plated to get an exact
nuance of expression in the color)
42" x 20.5" (107 cm x 52 cm)

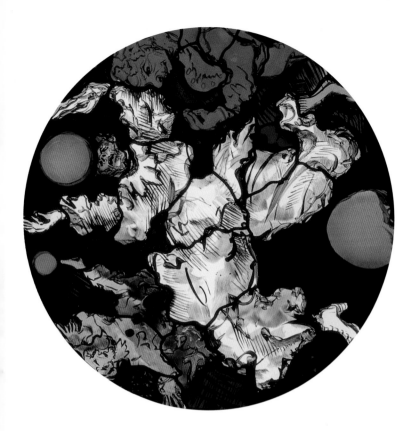

ONE OF EIGHT INDEPENDENT "CIRCUS" RONDELS
Ball Balance
German, French, and English antique glasses,
painted *alla prima* using matte and rapid brushstrokes
29" (74 cm) in diameter

ONE OF TWELVE WINDOWS
The Tenth Labor of Hercules
German, French, and English antique glasses,
painting and staining, with etching and plating
16.5" x 15" (42 cm x 38 cm)

ONE OF EIGHT INDEPENDENT "CIRCUS" RONDELS
A Pretty Balance
German, French, and English antique glasses,
painted *alla prima* using matte and rapid brushstrokes
29" (74 cm) in diameter

Ellen Mandelbaum

Ellen Mandelbaum's training and talent as a painter on canvas were essential to her development as a glass painter. She uses her grounding in traditional brushwork to explore the novel and varied ways glass and light can affect the viewer's perception of her painted images.

Glass art offers other attractions as well. Mandelbaum enjoys the physical act of working on a piece of glass. She finds that light passing through glass makes the experience different from painting on canvas or paper. Working with glass also gives her the chance to explore architectural considerations, something that has always interested her. And perhaps most important, with glass art, Mandelbaum has the opportunity to create a piece that intimately affects the work's owner; through this medium, she has discovered a level of personal contact she had not encountered before.

So almost from the start, Mandelbaum believed in the power of painted glass. Using a style ripe with nuance and inflected with almost constant references to nature, she creates art that truly matters. The honesty of each flowing brushstroke has a profound value and impact. To Mandelbaum, her work has the ability to transform simple light into a thing of greater beauty and to transform the lives of those who come in contact with it.

INDEPENDENT PANEL
MOUNTED IN WINDOW
Southampton Waves
Black paint, silk-screening,
reamy and antique glasses
21" x 46" (53 cm x 117 cm)

technique

Ellen Mandelbaum

One of my favorite parts of painting on glass is the actual painting, having the freedom of the brushstroke and being able to invent as I go. Traditionally, artists divide glass painting into matting and tracing, first putting down a general tone, and then creating a thin line. I do them together, which is a little more like regular painting in a way. But that is not to say that painting on glass is like painting on any other surface—it is a radically different thing. I love to put down tone and blend using a wide brush; then I scratch through and release the light. That part is so wonderful, and it is not like any other painting in the world.

The material itself is different as well. Glass paints are metal oxides. To use them, you mix in a little gum arabic—the same glue that holds watercolor together—and, in my case, some water.

I love the way glass paint flows over the surface of the glass, and I sometimes use reamy glass for this very effect. Painting is the one technique in which you really get a sense of the human touch. This is very evident in my work on *Grisaille Oval*, a piece I painted again and again. The painting was kind of pure and wonderful, and represents the potential for expression that exists in glass painting.

Ellen Mandelbaum

INDEPENDENT PANEL
Grisaille Oval
Grisaille brown, umber, black, and red
for flesh paints, on drawn antique glass
15" x 16" (38 cm x 41 cm)

WINDOW
Untitled
Black paint and silver stain, Fremont white-on-clear
wispy glass at center, French ruby glass, fluted glass
26" x 40" (66 cm x 102 cm)

ENTRYWAY SIDELIGHTS
(opposite and detail, left)
Untitled
Grisaille paints and silver
stain, antique glass
above, squares of
machine-rolled opales-
cent streaky glass below
16" x 70" (41 cm x 178 cm)
each

90

INDEPENDENT PANEL MOUNTED IN WINDOW
Wales Waterfall
Black and blue paint, antique blue and colored glasses
12" x 15" (30 cm x 38 cm)

INDEPENDENT PANEL
Imaginary Landscape
Black paint and ivory enamel, pure red, blue,
and light blue French mouthblown glasses
76" x 14" (193 cm x 36 cm)

ENTRYWAY SIDELIGHTS
Untitled
Grisaille paints and silver stain, antique glass
above, squares of machine-rolled opalescent
streaky glass below
16" x 70" (41 cm x 178 cm) each

Linda Lichtman's rich imagery challenges the viewer to shed traditional audience passivity

Linda Lichtman

and engage her vibrant choreography of dark jewel colors and assertive lines. Through her art, she strives to communicate a sense of the emotional content of her images.

The whipsaw movement and often surreal nature of Lichtman's luscious textural work invite intense exploration. Her painted glass art is driven by a palpable energy, a magical force derived from the balanced tension between openness and opacity, between the rigid framework of the lead line and the dynamic nature of Lichtman's brushwork.

INDEPENDENT PANEL
Snake in the Glass
Vitreous paint and silver stains, acid-etched stained glass
32" x 11" (81 cm x 28 cm)

That duality—between what is seen and what is not, between the physical and the spiritual, between compartments defined by lead lines and the free flow of imagery—adds life and vigor to Lichtman's work. Her commissions, such as *Tree of Knowledge*, *Tree of Light*, tend to be more transparent, with generous open areas. In contrast, her autonomous panels, such as *Primary Ties*, are more fluid, concentrated, and opaque. In both cases, Lichtman continually brings new and vital interpretations to the timeless technique of glass painting.

WINDOW
Family of Fish
Vitreous paint, enamels, and silver stains, acid-etched, laminated, and engraved stained glasses
43" x 13" (109 cm x 33 cm)

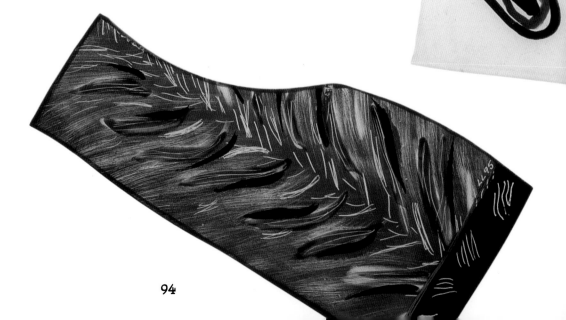

As beautiful as it is, stained glass, straight from the manufacturer, bores and challenges me. The excitement for me begins with tearing into the glass, whether with a Dremel engraver, acid etching, or paint. I can actually proceed almost as with a drawing, to have my hand in there making an imprint on the glass.

I like to literally and figuratively peel away a layer and reveal something underneath, which is why I often use flashed glass, where one color of glass is superimposed upon a layer of another color or clear glass. Acid etching flashed glass allows me to control how much of the color I leave on and how strong the color will be. Using acid in this way is almost another way to paint.

I like the fact that I'm using a material that can be seen as very rigid and cold—in a way, unresponsive and ungiving—and that I find ways of

making it more expressive and bending it to my
will. Some of this also has to do with my own
temperament. Spontaneity is a key to my
expressive style, and without it, I can become
quite frustrated. With painting and acid etching,
I get results that I am able to modify fairly easily.
Ultimately, I work to expand the possibilities
of the material itself, to penetrate and engage it
using the human touch and, thereby, to touch
the viewer.

95

Linda Lichtman

INDEPENDENT PANEL
Primary Ties
Vitreous paints and enamels, acid-etched and sandblasted
stained glasses, welded rebar and lead-wire frame
9" x 12" (23 cm x 30 cm)

LIBRARY WINDOW
Tree of Knowledge, Tree of Light
Vitreous paints, enamels, and silver stains,
acid-etched stained glass and float glass, leaded
and laminated
3.5' x 12' (1.1 m x 3.7 m)

96

INDEPENDENT PANEL (above)
Fish Flow, Lava Flow
Vitreous paints, acid-etched stained glass
22" x 12" (56 cm x 30 cm)

INDEPENDENT PANEL (below)
Waxing Germanic
Vitreous paints applied with wax resist,
acid-etched stained glass
16" x 12" (41 cm x 30 cm)

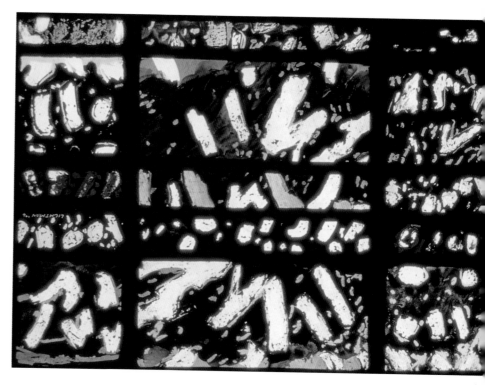

ONE OF SIX EXHIBITION PIECES (detail)
Six Land Escapes
Vitreous paints and enamels, acid-etched,
engraved, and laminated stained glasses,
steel wire and hardwood frame
36" x 8'4" (91 cm x 2.6 m)

Debora Coombs

Artist Debora Coombs has combined the seemingly incompatible worlds of precise, scientific geometry and warm, fluid organic form. Using the traditional technique of painting glass in most untraditional ways, Coombs creates artwork that invites the viewer to explore tier after tier of messages and meanings.

Coombs presents these meanings in many ways, ranging from semiabstract pieces to figural works to richly embellished geometric patterns. Regardless of the form, the spiritual dimension of her work and the humanity of her expressive painted lines cannot be denied.

Coombs's work possesses a metaphysical depth found both in the construction of each

EXHIBITION PIECE, IN THE COLLECTION OF
THE STAINED GLASS MUSEUM, ELY CATHEDRAL, ENGLAND
Out of Confusion . . .
Painted and stained glasses
78" x 52.5" (198 cm x 133 cm)

piece and in the often mathematical reasoning behind it. Coombs designed the window, *Out of Confusion . . .* based on the floor plan of St. Mary's Chapel in Glastonbury, Great Britain. She used this pattern to represent an internal narrative, with colors depicting emotions contained by black borders. Through this kind of art, Coombs elevates the glass painter's craft to the level of eternal and ethereal expression.

GALLERY EXHIBITION PIECE FROM THE SERIES "ONE WOMAN'S NARRATIVE," FROM THE COLLECTION OF CHRISTOPHER POWELL, ENGLAND
Blue Dog Daughters
Painted and stained glasses
15.5" x 23.25" (39 cm x 59 cm)

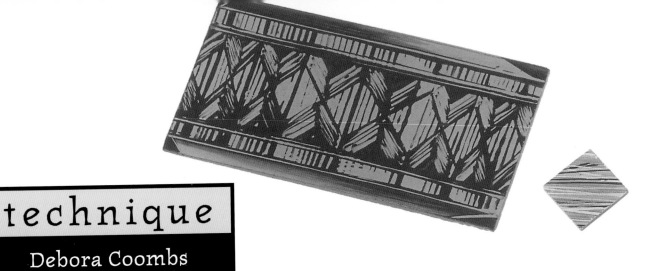

Glass painting has a centuries-old tradition in Europe, and I am always aware of that tradition, that I am working in a medium rich with history. Just the same, my own glass painting is extremely idiosyncratic. The style and manner of application are something that I've worked out myself through extensive experimentation.

Each new project challenges me to increase my repertoire of mark-making, my glass-painting vocabulary.

I like to get right into the paint. I find the material, the actual paint, very alluring. I often use my hands and get right in up to my elbows. I learned early on that you have to develop a certain immediacy and confidence with glass.

Glass painting can easily look like dirty smudges. You need good opacity, and you need to get it right the first time

so that the work has a sense of

spontaneity and liveliness.

I think we are all born with our own

"hand," our own innate style that develops and

matures over the years. Like calligraphy, glass

painting is something you do with your whole

mind and body; it is affected by the way you stand,

how you hold yourself, the way you breathe, and

the way gravity draws the paint down on the

brush. It's a fascinating balance of control of

the uncontrollable, which is certainly one of the

things I love best about painting on glass.

GALLERY EXHIBITION PIECE FROM THE SERIES
"ONE WOMAN'S NARRATIVE"
Self Portrait IV
Painted stained glass
12" x 8" (30 cm x 20 cm)

ENTRANCE FOYER WINDOW, ITCHEN COLLEGE
Ways of Seeing
Painted stained glass
3' 11" (.94 m) in diameter

STAINED GLASS WINDOW, WESTBOROUGH HIGH
SCHOOL, DEWSBURY, ENGLAND
Painted, stained, and clear textured glasses
9.1' x 17' (2.7 m x 5.2 m)

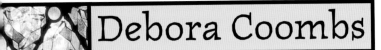

Debora Coombs

GALLERY EXHIBITION PIECE FROM THE SERIES
"ONE WOMAN'S NARRATIVE"
Collection of Dr. Gordon Bowe, Dublin, Ireland
Woman
Painted stained glass
15.5" x 23.25" (39 cm x 59 cm)

EXHIBITION PIECE
Inner Room
Painted stained glass
4.3' x 17" (1.3 m x 43 cm)

GALLERY EXHIBITION
PIECE FROM THE SERIES
"ONE WOMAN'S
NARRATIVE"
Young Willows . . .
Painted stained glass
15.5" x 23.25"
(39 cm x 59 cm)

Marie Foucault

Free spirit Marie Foucault challenges the traditions in which she was so thoroughly trained. A little over two decades ago, she graduated from the elite French National Superior School of Applied Arts and Crafts. She began a career as a highly regarded conservationist, a professional at restoring stained glass windows dating from the thirteenth to the sixteenth centuries. Although she achieved a mastery of antiquity, her passion lay in creating groundbreaking contemporary work.

Foucault willingly questions everything about her medium, including whether she needs to include lead lines. She works more and more on full sheets of clear and blown glasses, using a variety of paints to create what she would call "a new vocabulary." In a world where painted stained glass is poorly understood at best,

pushing the envelope of this form is risky. Yet Foucault has the faith of the talented.

Her confidence is apparent in every animated brushstroke and in every wild layer that forms an alliance with light. Foucault's work is fearless and overwhelming, so much a departure from her roots that you might think she has shed her past. But her beginnings set the stage for her current work. Foucault's creations represent a response to artistic freedom, celebrated in grand and glorious color and unrestrained line.

INDEPENDENT PANEL
Shroud
Blue grisaille, silver stain overfired, panel composed of six pieces of clear glass, painted on both sides and plated together to form a three-piece glass panel
20.25" x 21" (51 cm x 53 cm)

INDEPENDENT PANEL (opposite)
Tsunami
Blue and black grisaille on .25" plate glass
20" x 15" (51 cm x 38 cm)

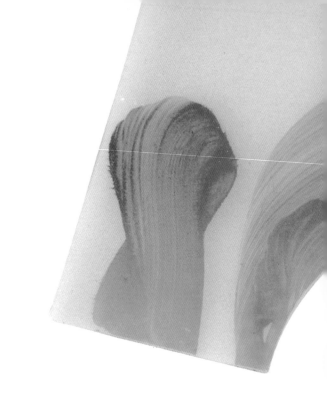

technique
Marie Foucault

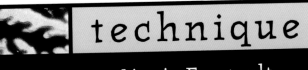

There is no escaping the fact that I learned

the techniques of painting and leaded

glasswork in a most traditional fashion.

My current work is indebted to the skills

I acquired in learning to do—and doing—

restoration work. But now I am willing

to try the unusual and look for possibilities

in everything. I hold no prejudices, even

about the material itself. I sometimes use

clear glass—chipped, scratched, damaged,

or found on the streets of New York. Suddenly, it is on the light table and under my brush, rich with grisaille paint, a new story being written. An area where my work is expanding is in the use of silver stains. In past centuries, stains were used on the back of glass to color areas of architecture, hair, draperies, and other fine details. Silver stain is generally fired at 1,050 degrees Fahrenheit. At higher temperatures, the silver in the stain "metalizes," creating a wild range of colors and iridescence. I love the iridescent quality, so I always fire my silver stain up to 1,150 or even 1,200 degrees Fahrenheit. As I use silver stain on the front of my work, the effect can be seen at night, with reflective light creating a completely different panel than the one seen during the day.

THREE SLIDING PANELS IN A SCREEN
Shadows of Reflection Triptych
Dark blue and white grisaille, orange silver
stain, French and German antique glasses
13' x 8'5" (4 m x 2.6 m)

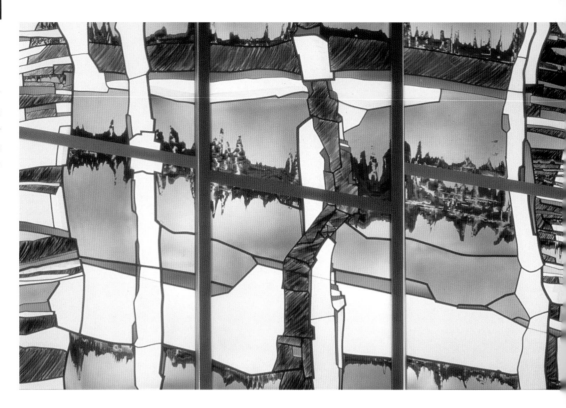

Marie Foucault

INDEPENDENT PANEL
Glass Kimono
Brown and black grisaille,
silver stain, clear window glass
15" x 20" (38 cm x 51 cm)

INDEPENDENT PANEL
Blue Damage
Blue and black grisaille, silver stain, clear restoration glass
21.5" x 18.5" (55 cm x 47 cm)

PANEL IN A
DOUBLE-HUNG WINDOW
The Cat and the Owl
Grisaille, French and
German antique glasses
48" x 35" (122 cm x 89 cm)

INDEPENDENT PANEL
FOR EXHIBITION
I Got the Blues
Blue and black grisaille,
silver stain, clear
window glass
12" (30 cm) square

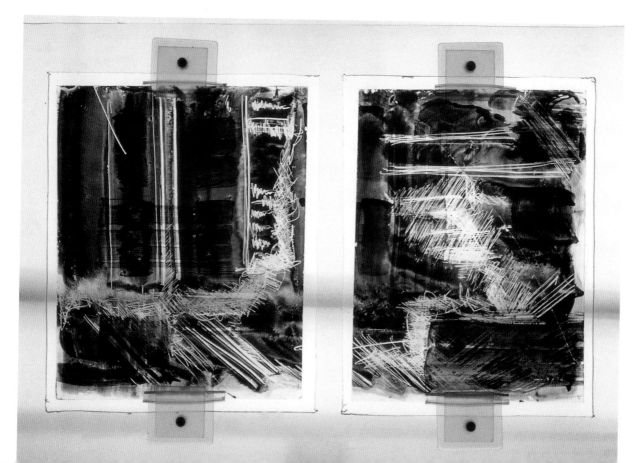

Irish artist Mary Mackey uses color as an ethereal

expression rather than as a tool. Her brilliant,

magical hues

become even

more radiant

when punctuated

by her kinetic line work. Her homeland serves as a

chief influence, specifically the dramatic lighting

and varied shades of Ireland.

Mackey first focused on the power of color

during her studies at Crawford College of Art and

Design in Ireland. After graduating as a painter,

she began to work in stained glass, a medium in

which she saw great potential. But her emphasis

on this medium does not mean she has left other

forms of painting behind. In fact, Mackey uses one

discipline to balance and support the other. Her

work with the same technique in different media

allows her to explore themes in various arenas.

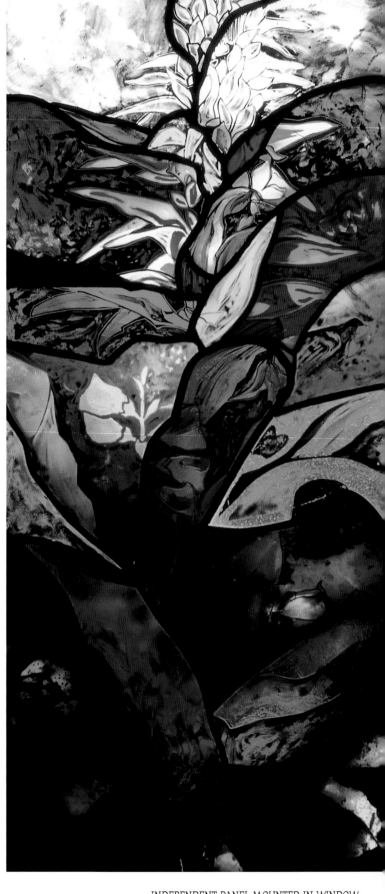

INDEPENDENT PANEL MOUNTED IN WINDOW
(above and detail, opposite)
Liquid Layers
Painted stained glass
17" x 38.5" (43 cm x 98 cm)

This interaction has led her to move from largely figural work to a more abstract vocabulary in her glass painting.

Mackey's recent work focuses less on structure and more on impressions and experience. Through her enigmatic use of color and layered shading and line, she attempts to communicate emotions and sensations. Removed from the perspective of literal imagery, she freely wanders through larger themes, exploring what the paint itself can contribute, and how best to orchestrate the timeless dance of intense color and vibrant light.

Acid etching is an essential technique

in my work, especially my more recent pieces.

Before I start, I have an idea of where I'm going

to etch, so that I do some areas quite strongly and

barely touch others. Generally, I leave the panel

unprotected and use a small dropper bottle to

squeeze a little acid in certain areas. I then spray

a little water on the panel to

push the acid out to the edge.

I will often selectively add drops

of more concentrated acid to give

subtle variations across the glass.

That's when I start to paint on it. I'll

start painting using large brushes and quite

wet pigment. I put the pigment on and let it dry,

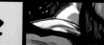

technique

Mary Mackey

and then blacken certain areas if I want the pigment to move a bit more. Then I let it dry and work into it with a badger brush or a smaller brush, emphasizing the movement taken by the wet pigment. Quite often, I leave it at that.

At other times, the panel requires a second working, so that the whole thing becomes layered; there will be a layer of the etching, a layer of the wet pigment and the dry one, and perhaps even a second firing. I often can't tell you in advance what I want; I just know in the doing. That versatility is one of the great things about painting.

113

INDEPENDENT PANEL
. . . and Flow
Painted stained glass
7" x 15" (18 cm x 38 cm)

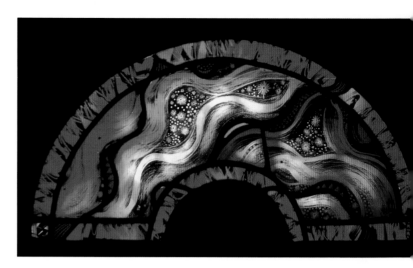

Mary Mackey

LIGHTBOX PANEL
Foxglove
Painted stained glass
15.5" x 12.5" (39 cm x 32 cm)

ENTRYWAY PANEL INSERTS
Moon over Minnane
Painted stained glass
2' x 3.5' (.6 m x 1.1 m)

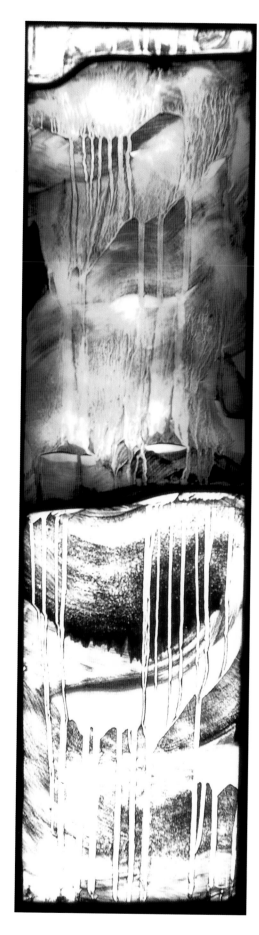

INDEPENDENT PANEL
In Contrast
Painted stained glass
16" x 13" (41 cm x 33 cm)

AUTONOMOUS PANEL FOR EXHIBITION
After Leenane
Painted stained glass
28" x 8" (71 cm x 20 cm)

FUSED GLASS
HOT HUES

Fusing represents an exciting and evolving addition to the glass artist's repertoire, one that returns the glass to the heat from which it was born. The process involves bonding one glass to another with intense heat. An artist must master this highly technical procedure to be able to translate a creative vision into a finished piece. However, the results can be incredibly stunning: shapes have dimension and definition, colors pop dramatically, and the glass surface holds a remarkable luster.

Richard LaLonde has developed exceptional technical refinements to create his wall-mounted murals. Once crafted, his designs evoke the drama of the human connection to the natural world, to spiritual and mystical dimensions, and to the past, present, and future. Liz Mapelli also creates wall-mounted works, ranging from mini-canvases of small fused tiles to larger pieces that dominate the spaces they inhabit. Mapelli breaks with convention to create abstract designs in hot-worked glass.

Brilliant colors and inviting textures characterize Maya Radoczy's fused and cast-glass artworks. She brings a fresh, exciting, and vibrant style to each new piece she creates. Judy Gorsuch Collins has also created a signature style, one that combines the playful with the practical. Her panels incorporate fused and traditional stained glass pieces to joyful effect. The result is a dynamic and fun-loving marriage of techniques that amplifies the best of both.

Judy Gorsuch Collins
INDIVIDUAL FUSED TILES, ST. ANNE'S SCHOOL
INSTALLATION (detail, right and opposite)
Tiles of stained glass fused on etched glass,
stained glass adjoining
4" x 4" (10 cm x 10 cm) each tile

It's no accident that Richard LaLonde found his creative voice in the kiln-fired milieu of fused

Richard LaLonde

glass—his artistic exploration began with heat. Using a welding torch, he began his career creating metal sculptures within the traditions of the craft movement of the early 1970s. LaLonde eventually found the medium stifling and went in search of greater color and artistic possibilities. That search ultimately led him to the growing culture of fused glass artistry.

Over the next two decades, LaLonde experimented, tested, and refined the process of fusing to serve his own artistic needs. Along the way, he pioneered techniques that were essential to creating his signature style.

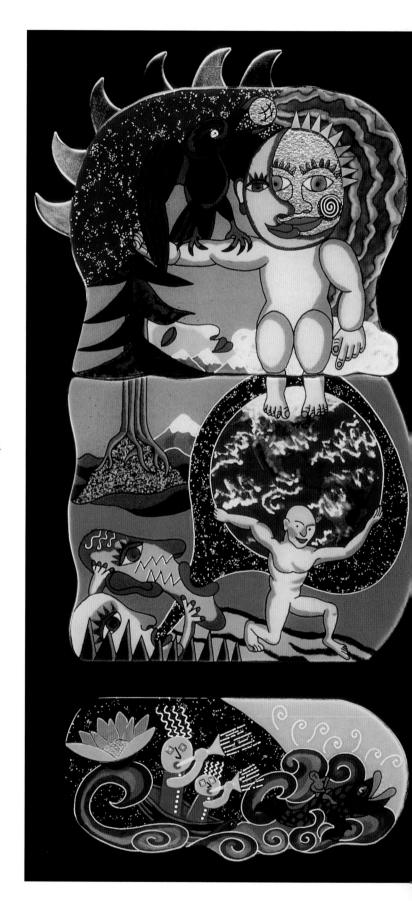

WALL MURAL
Mystic Messenger
Crushed colored glasses fused on clear glass
56" x 28" (142 cm x 71 cm)

His work is at once mysterious and obvious, a celebration of life in all its bright colors and an exploration of the mystery that lies beyond. These dualities echo throughout his pieces, in themes that juxtapose male and female, hard and soft, internal and external. He draws from a variety of cultures—from Native American to Guatemalan Indian—to create his own artistic mythology. And, just as LaLonde would have it, viewers can bring their own meanings and interpretations to this mythology and take away what means most to them.

WALL MURAL
Remember There Are Stars in the Sky
Crushed colored glasses fused on clear glass
52" x 76" (132 cm x 193 cm)

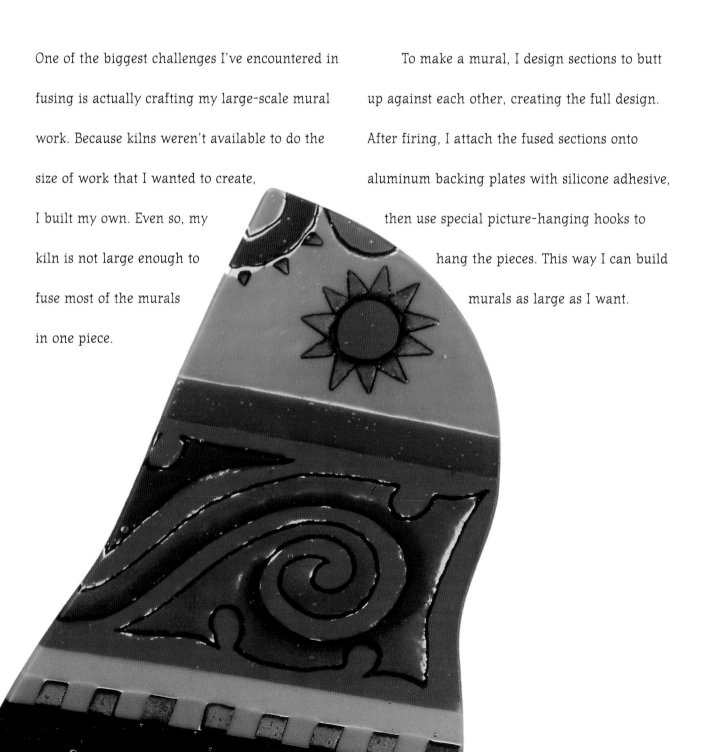

One of the biggest challenges I've encountered in fusing is actually crafting my large-scale mural work. Because kilns weren't available to do the size of work that I wanted to create, I built my own. Even so, my kiln is not large enough to fuse most of the murals in one piece.

To make a mural, I design sections to butt up against each other, creating the full design. After firing, I attach the fused sections onto aluminum backing plates with silicone adhesive, then use special picture-hanging hooks to hang the pieces. This way I can build murals as large as I want.

technique

Richard LaLonde

Another breakthrough was the use of crushed glass. Originally, I cut glass pieces and used them in much the same way you would in a stained glass window. But I wanted more freedom to use the color in a vibrant and fluid way, so I began using glass crushed to the consistency of table sugar. I pour it out in the design on the back of a piece of super clear glass (glass with no green tint to it). I then use a brush to "tone" up the line of the crushed glass. Finally, I tamp it down with a spoon, then fire the piece. This method has allowed for a lot of spontaneity, which adds to the unique character of my work.

WALL MURAL (left)
I Dream of Flying
Crushed, colored
glass fused onto
a clear sheet
54" x 66"
(137 cm x 168 cm)

Richard LaLonde

WALL MURAL (left)
Touch
Crushed, colored glass
fused onto a clear sheet
62" x 56" (157 cm x 142 cm)

WALL MURAL (right)
The Four Elements
Crushed, colored glass fused
onto a clear sheet
52" x 84" (132 cm x 213 cm)

WALL MURAL
The Hand of Humankind
Crushed, colored glass fused
onto a clear sheet
74" x 90" (188 cm x 229 cm)

WALL MURAL
World View
Crushed, colored glass fused
onto a clear sheet
43" x 66" (109 cm x 168 cm)

From the beginning of her career, Liz Mapelli

has explored an unusual and dynamic new way

Liz Mapelli

of utilizing

glass. Her

large-format

commissions

rely on the sense of depth inherent in the surface

of fused glass. They are designed to be viewed in

reflected rather than transmitted light, setting

them apart from most other forms of stained

glass art.

Mapelli's introduction to the technique of

fused glass was as unusual as her style, through

working in the front office of a pioneering glass

company in Portland, Oregon. The company,

Bullseye Glass, was the leader in the emerging

arena of fused glass art, experimenting with

techniques and compatible glasses. Mapelli was

soon drawn to the unique and tactile qualities

intrinsic to fused layers of glass.

She began by fusing small autonomous

pieces, but broke through to create a larger

commission for the Portland Justice Center. From that starting point, she pursued large architectural commissions exclusively, projects that would allow her the range of expression she desired.

Impressive size is the first feature to attract attention to her work, drawing the viewer near. But upon closer inspection, Mapelli's fine detailing becomes apparent. Brilliant swirls, cubes, and chunks of vivid, shiny color seem to pop right off the surface. The magic of Mapelli's art resides in this transition from the large, unified design down to the amazing individual details that form the design.

WALL-MOUNTED TILES,
SUMNER ARTS CENTER (opposite and detail, above)
Fused and enameled stained glasses
30' x 4' (9.1 m x 1.2 m)

technique

Liz Mapelli

I work almost exclusively on large, architectural commissions. They bring with them many difficulties that have to be dealt with for the piece to remain intact and have lasting beauty. Many of these challenges relate to the details of the installation. A few years ago, I worked on a project to be installed in Colorado, where the climate was much less humid than where my studio is located in Oregon. I had glued the fired glass panels onto tempered Masonite, and when the piece got to Colorado, the glue shrank and all the glass broke. It was 6 feet by 42 feet (1.8 meters by 12.8 meters) of broken glass. I had to remake the entire project. Now, that's a learning experience.

To create large commissions, you need to have an organized, well-run studio. I work closely

with the architectural team on all projects. I work with a felt-tipped pen on transparent paper to develop a general concept. Then I start working with panels of glass testing out colors. From there, I lay out the piece full-scale and draw the imagery directly onto the glass. I start working enamels over the top, layering until I'm ready to start firing.

I think after fifteen years, I'm more realistic about the things I propose to do, but I still have a need to do new sorts of projects and try new techniques. Each project has its own, sometimes painful, learning curve.

WALL-MOUNTED SECTIONAL PIECES
Aloha Grotto
Fused and enameled stained glasses
9' x 11' (2.7 m x 3.4 m)

WALL MURAL (detail)
Memorial To Police And Fire
Fused and enameled stained glasses, stainless steel
14' x 16' (4.3 m x 4.9 m)

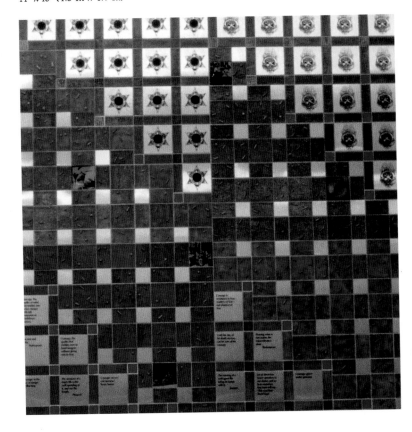

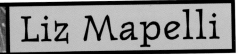

Liz Mapelli

WALL-MOUNTED SECTIONS
Galaxies–Peace Plaza
Fused and enameled stained glasses
25' x 4' (7.6 m x 1.2 m)

ONE IN A SERIES OF INDIVIDUAL
DECORATIVE TILES (detail)
Space Series Tile
Fused glass, enamels
8" x 8" (20 cm x 20 cm)

Bright and modern, Maya Radoczy's glass art represents a tour de force of fusing and casting.

Maya Radoczy

Her pieces are characteristically bright and playful, with stimulating colors set against a predominance of clear and textured glasses. Her work often incorporates textural elements, adding a sculptural dimension and maintaining the relationship of the glass to light.

Given her initial work in leaded glass, Radoczy's affinity for hot-glass techniques is somewhat surprising. After art school, she apprenticed at an eminent stained glass studio in Germany. There, she spent long, intense days studying painting, *dalle de verre*, restoration techniques, and other mainstays of leaded glasswork.

She might have stayed with leaded glass if she had not physically moved into the heart of

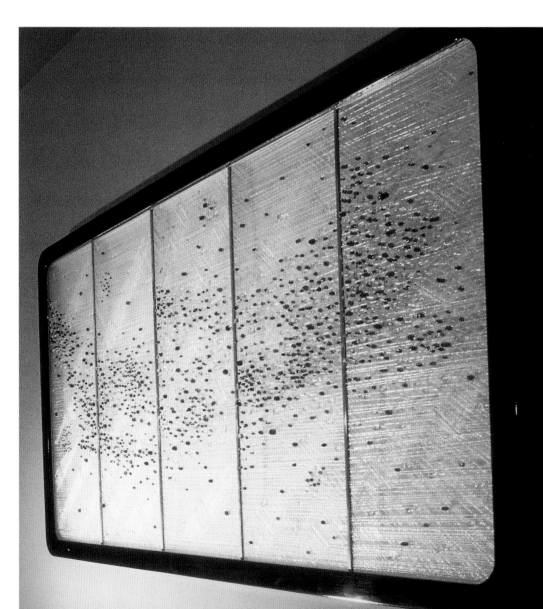

MOUNTED WALL SCULPTURE
(right and detail, opposite)
Fused glass
3' x 6' (.9 m x 1.8 m)

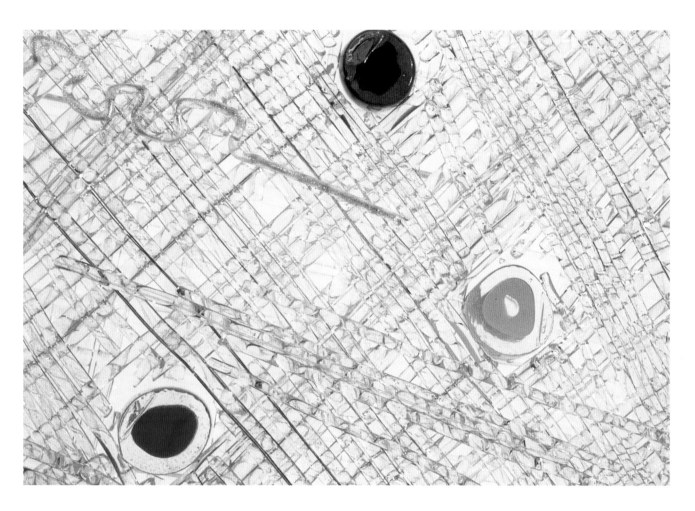

the emerging fused glass movement in Seattle, Washington. It may be that fusing–spontaneous, active, energetic, and charismatic–matched her artistic style.

Drawing from a platform of balance and clarity, Radoczy's work builds with a force akin to disparate atoms spinning as a unified whole. Her designs are formed from the combination of structures, making the finished pieces fascinating both from afar and up close. Radoczy's art inhabits a cheerful, lively galaxy that is as rewarding to the spirit as it is to the eye.

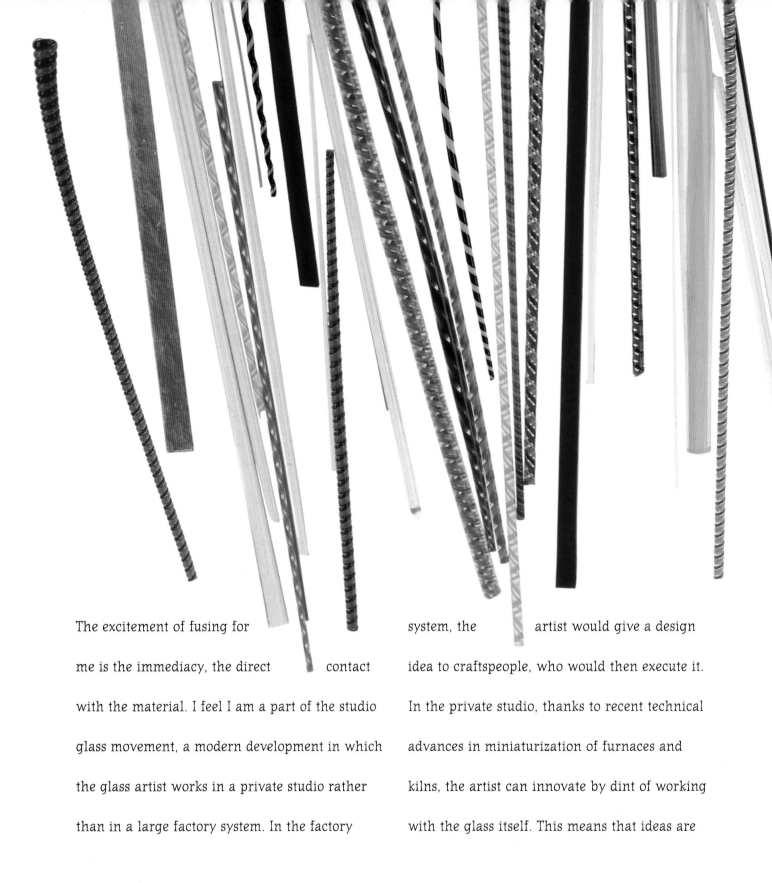

The excitement of fusing for me is the immediacy, the direct contact with the material. I feel I am a part of the studio glass movement, a modern development in which the glass artist works in a private studio rather than in a large factory system. In the factory system, the artist would give a design idea to craftspeople, who would then execute it. In the private studio, thanks to recent technical advances in miniaturization of furnaces and kilns, the artist can innovate by dint of working with the glass itself. This means that ideas are

technique
Maya Radoczy

not only coming from the sketch pad, but from the very process of working with the material.

I started fusing as soon as I moved to Seattle. I learned to blow, cast, and fuse glass. I sometimes use a combination of these to create an artwork. For example, I will take glass of a certain color and pull it into a rod. Then I will take the rod and put it onto another piece of glass, fuse them, cut them, and wind up with a varied, textured piece of glass. By combining techniques in this way, I can be quite painterly with the material.

DOOR PANELS,
REI LANDMARK BUILDING
24 hand-cast panels
11" x 17" (28 cm x 43 cm) each

Maya Radoczy

DOOR PANELS, REI LANDMARK BUILDING
(detail showing single panel with glacier image)

GLASS SCREEN FOR WINDOW
Fused and leaded handblown glasses
3.6' x 6.5' (1.1 m x 2 m)

MOBILE, CLERESTORY TOWER IN SCHOOL LIBRARY
Cast glass and metal tubing
3' x 6' (.9 m x 1.8 m)

Judy Gorsuch Collins first became aware of the power of stained glass while living in an older

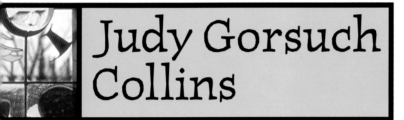

Judy Gorsuch Collins

house in Colorado with a traditional stained glass window that enchanted her. But in her artistic explorations, the less-traditional technique of

fusing held the most fascination. Her graphic design background had found a new means of expression, one that seemed perpetually fresh.

She most often articulates that expression in complicated architectural commissions that combine aesthetic requirements with a strong emotional or personal element. Typical is the Denver's Children's Museum glass wall. Built for hearing- and sight-impaired children, the glass

wall includes colored, clear, and textured glasses, unusual optical effects, and even metal disc knock-knock jokes in Braille. This playful, dynamic design embodies the tactile sense that forms so much of the attraction of art glass— the panels are meant to be touched as much as viewed.

Each of Collins's commissions possesses this sensitivity to the audience. She creates designs with color and texture that are appropriate to the space, but that also meet the more individualized ephemeral and cerebral needs of those who interact with the artwork. What remains constant for Collins, however, is her desire that the experience of the art, both in its creation and in its viewing, be rewarding for artist and audience alike.

GLASS WALL, DENVER CHILDREN'S MUSEUM
(opposite and detail, right)
Fused clear and stained glasses, machine glass,
painting, sandblasting
8' x 20' (2.4 m x 6.1 m)

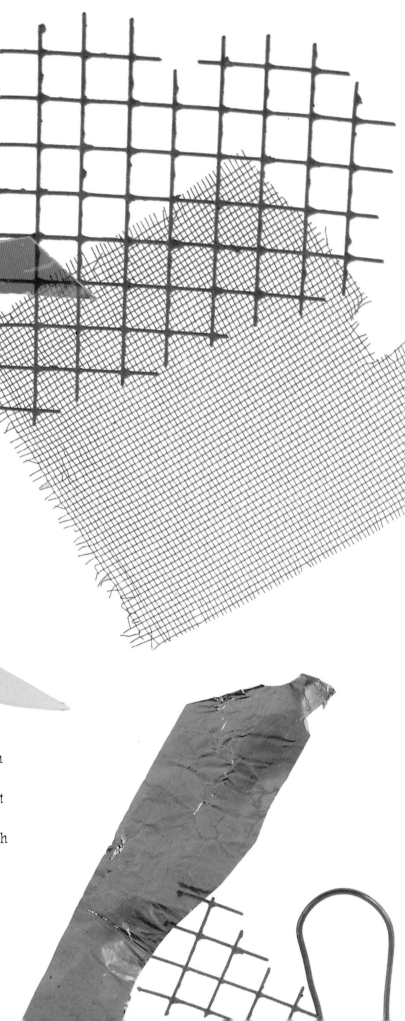

technique

Judy Gorsuch Collins

I really enjoy problem-solving, which is
a constant in my commissions. I look
to challenge myself with each commission,
because I want to do something new and
different every time. You can be incredibly
accurate technically, using compatible glasses
and annealing to scientific precision,
but you will still be
surprised sometimes. There
are always variables, and the
trick is to use them to your advantage.

    I discovered this through experience, when
I fired a sheet of double-rolled glass onto a sheet
of single-rolled. Air bubbles were trapped, which
would usually be an unpleasant surprise. But I

have recently incorporated this unique effect in a commission to achieve an original and pleasing look.

In fact, it is no longer the errors in glass I worry about. At this point, I am confident of my skill in getting the glass to do what I want. I use a custom-built kiln and a computerized controller, so it is rare that things go wrong. It is in new materials that I'm looking for mystery and excitement.

My most recent explorations involve using metal as a partner to the fused glass. I have been layering metals between glass sheets and firing. I've found that one time the metal will do one thing and another time it will do something entirely different. Wherever this new work takes me, I'm fairly certain that new surprises are right around the corner.

COFFEE TABLE
Fused glass
4' x 2.5' (1.2 m x .8 m)

Judy Gorsuch Collins

WALL MURAL, CORPORATE OFFICE (detail)
Fused clear and colored glasses, enamels
10' x 3' (3 m x .9 m)

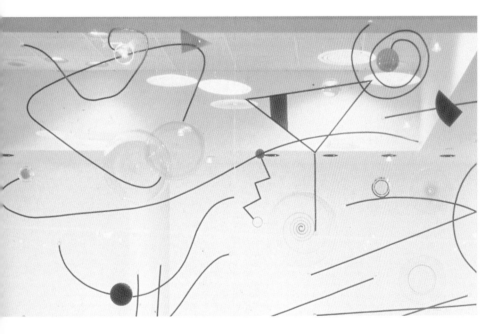

INTERIOR GLASS WALL, RESTAURANT (detail)
Fused, laminated, stained, and clear glasses
5' x 40' (1.5 m x 12.2 m)

DOOR AND WINDOW, OFFICE ENTRYWAY
Enameled and laminated glasses
11' x 6' (3.4 m x 1.8 m)

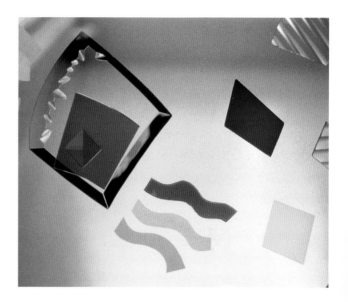

WINDOW, OFFICE ENTRYWAY (detail)

TILED GYMNASIUM
BREEZEWAY AND ENTRYWAY,
ST. ANNE'S EPISCOPAL SCHOOL
Fused glass tiles
240 square feet (21.6 square meters),
each tile 7" x 7" (18 cm x 18 cm)

directory of artists

Sigrídur Asgeirsdóttir
Dràpuhlid 13
105 Reykjavík
Iceland
Phone: (354) 551 1031

Debora Coombs
RR 1, Box 531
Reedsboro, VT 05350
Phone: (802) 423-5869
Fax: (802) 423-5869

Marie Pascale Foucault-Phipps
The Quarter Circle Bell Ranch
41348 Road 29
Elizabeth, CO 80107
Phone: (303) 646-4784
Fax: (303) 646-4765

Judy Gorsuch Collins
8283 West Iliff Lane
Lakewood, CO 80227
Phone: (303) 985-8081
Fax: (303) 980-0692

Lutz Haufschild
Gotthard Strasse 26
8800 Thalwil
Switzerland
Phone: (41) 1722-11-38
Fax: (41) 1722-11-38

Virginia Hoffman
P.O. Box 2712
Sarasota, FL 34230
Phone: (941) 365-7450

Shelley Jurs
4167 Wilshire Boulevard
Oakland, CA 94602
Phone: (510) 521-7765
Fax: (510) 531-6173

Kuni Kajiwara
1996-1 Oturumachi
Hita-City, Oita-Ken
Japan
Phone: (81) 973-28-2105
Fax: (81) 973-28-2626

Richard LaLonde
4651 South Melody Lane
Freeland, WA 98249
Phone: (360) 730-2166
Fax: (360) 730-2151

Linda Lichtman
17 Tudor Street
Cambridge, MA 02139
Phone: (617) 876-4660
Fax: (617) 354-1119

Mary Mackey
Coachman's House
Laurel Walk
Bandon, County Cork
Ireland
Phone: (353) 23-44402

Ellen Mandelbaum
39-49 46th Street
Long Island City, NY 11104
Phone: (718) 361-8154
Fax: (718) 361-8154

Liz Mapelli
P.O. Box 3885
Portland, OR 97208
Phone: (503) 796-0221

Rick Melby
37 Biltmore Avenue
Asheville, NC 28801
Phone: (704) 232-0905

Carl Powell
1610 Ninth Street
Berkeley, CA 94710
Phone: (510) 526-2637

Maya Radoczy
P.O. Box 31422
Seattle, WA 98103
Phone: (206) 527-5022
Fax: (206) 524-9226

Patrick Reyntiens
Ilford Bridges Farm
Close Stocklinch
Ilminster, Somerset
Great Britain
Phone: (44) 1460-52241
Fax: (44) 1460-57150

Rachel Schutt-Mesrahi
50 Oak Knoll Avenue
San Anselmo, CA 95960
Phone: (415) 454-8537
Fax: (415) 721-0607

Kenneth vonRoenn
1110 Baxter Avenue
Louisville, KY 40204
Phone: (502) 585-5421
Fax: (502) 585-2808

David Wilson
202 Darby Road
South New Berlin, NY 13843
Phone: (607) 334-3015

Larry Zgoda
2117 West Irving Park Road
Chicago, IL 60618
Phone: (773) 463-3970
Fax: (773) 463-3978

*For further information
on the history and the art
of stained glass, contact the
following organizations.*

The Stained Glass Association
of America
P.O. Box 22642
Kansas City, MO 64113
Phone: (800) 888-7422
Fax: (816) 361-9173

The Stained Glass Museum
10 Ferry Lane
Chesterton, Cambridge CB4 1NT
Great Britain
Phone: (44) 01223 327367
Fax: (44) 01223 327367

The Corning Museum of Glass
One Museum Way
Corning, NY 14830
Phone: (607) 937-5371
Fax: (607) 937-3352

photography credits

Debora Coombs

Out of Confusion,
Inner Room,
Young Willows . . ., and
Woman from the series
"One Woman's Narrative,"
Collection of Dr. Gordon Bowe,
Dublin, Ireland
Photos by Brian Nash

Ways of Seeing
Photo by Robin Paskins

Stained Glass Window,
Westborough High School,
Dewsbury, England
Photo by Paul Schatzberger

Lutz Haufschild

Spectra Veil Sample and
Blue Heart
Fabricated by Wilhelm Derix
Studios, Taunusstein, Germany

The Four Seasons, Gl/ass, The Fire
Fighting Window, and
Time and Space
Photos by Lutz Haufschild

Tribute to Baseball
Photo by Otto Bierwagen

Richard LaLonde

Mystic Messenger,
World View,
The Four Elements,
I Dream of Flying,
The Hand of Humankind,
and *Touch*
All photos by Roger Schreiber

Kenneth vonRoenn

Doors, Glass Sculptural
Column
Photos by Mike Robertson

Entryway
Photo by John Beckman/
Quadrant Photography

David Wilson

Window, Nation's Bank,
Dichroic Glass Doors (page 20),
and Window (page 21, top)
Photos by Kevin Roche,
John Dinkeloo & Associates,
Architects

Creation Window,
Beth David Congregation
Photo by Shapiro, Petrauskas
Gelber, Architects

Window (page 21, bottom)
Photo by Cass & Associates,
Architects

Barrel Vault Window,
St. Paul's Catholic Church
Photo by The Ashford Group,
Architects

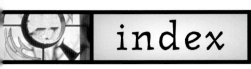

index